From the Cartel to Christ

How God Restores Stolen Dreams

By

Jack E. Rausch

FROM THE CARTEL TO CHRIST

First printing January 2014

Cover by Lisa Hainline Design www.LionsgateBookDesign.com

ISBN-10: 0991380703
ISBN-13: 978-0-9913807-0-1

DEDICATION

To my mom: I am sorry for all I made you suffer.

To my son Jack Sebastian: I pray that you follow Jesus.

CONTENTS

Part One. The Cartel.

Part Two. Christ.

My love goes to Pastor Chuck Smith, Pastor Neil Travisano, Pastor Gerson Hernandez, Pastor John Randall, and all the other pastors and teachers that molded me and continue to contribute to make me the man of God I am.

To Chip MacGregor from MacGregor Literary, Inc. and Elizabeth M. Thompson, thanks for the 1st Place Nonfiction Award at the 2012 Write to Inspire Conference.

To Lisa Hainline, for the cover design, good job!

To Michelle Massaro, thanks for your help with the editing.

To Cecil Murphey I am grateful for your support.

Thanks to all my teachers and guides through this journey, I know it took lots of patience.

God bless you all.

To all people affected by drug trafficking I am sorry for my actions. I pray that you all seek God for healing.

Thanks for your interest in my book.
I appreciate your review at Amazon.com
From the Cartel to Christ.
Any comments and imput, typos and suggestions
please e-mail me: jackerausch@yahoo.com
God bless

1 THE RUNWAY TO HELL

Too excited to be scared, I held my semi-automatic pistol and looked around. Anything could happen. My average size, smaller gun, and inexperience, forced me to be on my toes.

The heat and humidity, typical of northern Colombia, loaded the late morning. I could taste the sweat, and it stung my eyes making me irritable. The thin shirt stuck to my back like a second skin. But the musky scent of the vegetation had a calming effect, distracting my conscience by the beauty of the surrounding nature.

Waiting under the tall trees by the end of the clandestine runway, my team partner sat on the idling farm tractor while I perched on the big canvas bags holding the kilos of cocaine that layered the rusted trailer. The singing crickets kept rhythm with my heart. A mosquito landed on my arm and started feeding, getting my prompt attention. I slapped the pest. "There you go, sucker." I wiped off the bloody carcass. My partner turned and put the index finger to his lips.

Time dragged as I dreamt of an ice cold beer.

Suddenly, an eerie silence fell over the jungle and the

handheld radio crackled "The plane. The plane. Go. Go. Go."

The twin engine aircraft zoomed over the trees in an attempt to avoid detection by the police of the nearby town, buying a few minutes to complete the operation. The roaring sent a rush of adrenaline through my veins. Like a bull hit by a cattle prod, my brain cells exploded into action.

My partner gunned the engine and the tractor jumped forward. I shoved the gun into my waistband and clung to the bags. We bounced over the tree roots and bushes, until we emerged into the clearing of the runway.

I scanned the area for any sign of trouble. Guerrilla, paramilitary groups, police, or military patrols, could appear at any time.

The plane hummed at the end of the runway with the right engine running. In the cockpit, the pilot looked around as the co-pilot stepped out and jumped on top of the left wing. The fueling crew's tractor stopped by and they rushed to refuel the plane.

The shipper's representative, lean and tall, with thick black mane flowing in the wind, stood on the roof of his SUV holding an Uzi machine gun yelling orders.

What am I doing here? He could kill us as soon as the plane leaves...

The two guys who brought the merchandise on a small truck had dropped it and left. God only knew who else had knowledge of this going down today. Live fast and die faster.

We halted by the side of the airplane.

"Quickly, quickly, get it loaded at once." The shipper waved the machine gun from us to the plane, as if we needed direction and additional incentive.

The fueling crew finished and drove away. I passed the bags to my partner and he passed them on to the copilot, who had climbed into the plane. The whole operation was completed in minutes. We jumped back on the tractor and sped back under the trees.

I turned and saw the copilot close the door. The other engine roared to life as the plane turned and aligned with the runway. If I were the pilot, I would have turned it before the loading, in case I had to fly out in the middle of the operation.

Engines screaming, the plane shook, jumped, and picked up speed. Heavy, it ran, ran and ran. The hot thin air of the late morning provided less lift. It took most of the runway to lift off.

Luckily, the long runway sloped down with no trees at the end. The plane finally lifted and flew out of sight. I watched it go, like an old girlfriend walking away on the arm of a better suitor.

As a newly licensed pilot, I wanted to fly, anything, for anybody. I craved what I didn't have, blinded to believe the life of that pilot was better than mine. For all I knew, they could have been shot down by an Air Force jet, or run out of fuel, or arrested on delivery, or killed by the receiving crew to keep the load. But there I was, wishing on the wind.

Cartel pilots got rich quick, and died quicker.

We hid the tractor and trailer back into the bushes, ran to our SUV, and raced into the jungle. My partner drove, and in some places I couldn't even see the trail because of the vegetation covering it. We sped through, splashing and fishtailing, until we emerged onto the highway where we joined tourists, farmers, and probably other crews coming and going to keep the trade in motion. The cocaine trade machine ran on blood and millions.

Now it was payday, celebration time. We went to a pizzeria in town and the boss paid me one hundred thousand pesos about three hundred dollars in the early 1980s, still, a lot of money for a couple of days' work. Holding my fattened handbag on my lap I felt a rush of pride, not only because of the money, but because I was *in the big game*. Yes, I was in it to get rich, but I also wanted to belong, be a part of something. I looked forward to the next operation already.

I observed the people in the restaurant. I felt exposed. Was it obvious I was a Mafioso now? *I want the money but not to look tacky...What's my family going to think of me now? Well, I am the Black Sheep anyway...Who cares? What family? What am I doing here?*

These events in the jungle lead to a major turning point in my life. Fifteen years later it all came to an end, this journey of fantasies and dreams, lies and deceit, death and destruction, this journey ends in prison.

Living the lie, led me to face the Truth.

How did it all start? How did it all end?

2 THE INFLUENCE

I'd been sleeping in dad's bed the night he told mom he was leaving us. I woke up when he came in the room but pretended to sleep. He lay on top of my small-seven-year-old frame as he slurred his leaving speech. The misty cloud of alcohol and tobacco made my stomach turn and all I could think about was for him to go away.

A few months later, Mom took my older sister and me, and we moved to Medellín where her family lived. I missed a father figure, but not his drunken outbursts, nor his "you eat it or wear it." He'd smeared the oatmeal on my face once for not wanting to eat it. His military academy's discipline terrified me.

I had nightmares about him for years.

Life went on just fine without a father. Love and hate. I wished to have a perfect dad, at home, not violent, not a drunk.

He'd rose from a messenger position at the local bank to director of agricultural loans. Then, he quit his job and bought a patch of jungle in northern Colombia by the Gulf of Urabá. His project made me proud. Turning the 250 acres of jungle into a year-round producing plantation represented a process of humongous proportion. Carving the road and getting to the area appeared like a scene from an Indiana Jones movie. Yet, it took years and thousands of man hours, but he built it and produced hundreds of boxes of bananas a week for the American markets. He also managed four other plantations belonging to powerful friends, doctors, executives, and politicians, Colombia's high society. They usually came to the area on vacation with their families, and so did I.

It was there where I got the worst beating of my life.

My father, sister —on a rare school vacation visit- and I went to a barbeque at Gustavo's plantation.

The hacienda, just a driveway and parking lot to the occasional driver-by, spoiled all its visitors. A big room with comfortable chairs and sofas along with a Ping-Pong table led to the dining room and kitchen, featuring to the left an independent apartment with private bathroom. Nothing special until a dark fancy wood door opened to the next area. The air conditioned exotic paradise contrasted with the hellish humidity behind me. The kid's three-bed room connected to the royal spread filled with plush leather couches and oversized chairs that filled my nostrils with that intoxicating aroma of power and money. A marble bathroom suited for a roman king opened to the left, an area I only entered once, invited by Gustavo to wash my hands. Near the back wall a desk and seating area with a long table covered with aviation magazines that upon exploration uncovered the Playboy's breath-taking glossy apparitions. A spiral staircase led to a loft fitted with a bed for six. A double door to the terrace and swimming pool area finished the overwhelming tour. I never wanted to leave.

He was one of my father's employers, and his best friend. While there, all the kids, including my sister and me, went to play at the packing plant. After a while, my sister went to the bathroom at the main house. When I came back, my father asked me where she was. I didn't know. He transformed, his blue eyes bulged, and his face turned red.

My heart thumped wildly when he unclasped his belt buckle, and slid it out from the loops. In a flash, he raised his muscled arm, and sent the belt cracking across my back as I turned and covered my face with my arms.

"You're supposed to know where she is at all times." Crack. Crack. His belt burned on my back.

I am only twelve years old. Why should I be her guardian? She is three years older than I.

Crack. Crack. The belt hit, and hit…

"Jack, stop-" Gustavo yelled.

"No, he has to learn..." My father slurred.

"No, it's enough." Gustavo pulled him away. My father was strong, but Gustavo was build like a bear.

"Come…come with me Jack…let's have another drink." Mike, another friend, walked my father to the bar.

"Mono, let's go… it's going to be ok." Gustavo gently led me away and into the apartment at the front of the hacienda.

Everyone still called me *Mono,* blond, because as a baby, my hair was light colored, even though it'd turned brown.

"Why does he hit me like that?" I sobbed. "It hurts so… bad…"

He put his hand on my back.

"Ouch. That hurts." I pulled away.

Gustavo sat on the bed and held me in front of him. "Let me see." His big face, topped with a military haircut, stood just a few inches from mine as he unbuttoned my shirt and took it off.

My sister and other kids came into the room.

"Wow, his back is…is turning black and blue!" One of the kids exclaimed and recoiled.

My sister just stood there.

"He is bleeding…" Another said.

Gustavo shushed them away.

"It's not fair..." I cried.

Gustavo's wife came in the room with a glass of water. "Here take these." She handed me a couple of pills and stood by my side.

They laid me down on the bed and covered me with a sheet. "Rest, we'll check on you later." Gustavo said.

I stared at the window and cried myself to sleep.

Gustavo, from a powerful family from Bogotá, piloted a twin-engine plane for the exporting company. His rifles, shotguns, and handguns inspired fear, power, and awe. His brother, a politician, his two sons Rodrigo, my age, and Mauricio, a couple of years younger, along with his wife and older daughter appeared to me like the aristocratic families seen on TV. He was as close to my hero as anyone could ever be.

My dad enjoyed cooking at his parties. One day, at another barbeque at his house, his sons and I were wrestling in their room as Gustavo passed by and joined us. Something was wrong with the way he grabbed and squeezed me. I felt dirty but didn't know why.

The future held a horrible revelation.

Vacation times came and went, and life continued its running path.

***

In Medellín, the second-largest city in Colombia, mom got an apartment in el barrio Los Angeles, northwest of downtown. I attended the Calasanz, a Catholic school, and performed well as a student.

Family gatherings were especially stressful for my mother because of my mischief. Once, we attended a wedding at my uncle's Spanish style mansion in El Poblado, the best area of Medellín at that time. I often visited the huge home with its magnificent entrance, explored the different rooms, the oak paneled library with plush leather chairs and sofas, the garages, maids' chambers, and basement rooms with their distinctive moldy smell. I ran around the expansive backyard and picked *zapotes,* a delicious tropical fruit. Or, I watched from a distance the dog pens with purebred boxers waiting anxiously to be freed at night to devour unwanted visitors.

At the wedding, I wandered around the kitchen and into the pantry to find a table covered with desserts. They were delicious. Later, when the guests finished the meal, twenty four of them had to go without a sweet treat.

My mother nagged me about it for years. "Remember the time when you ate all the desserts at…"

Poor mom, I gave her such a hard time.

But, family gatherings weren't all sweet and happy times for me.

One Christmas, when I was about ten years old, we gathered at Aunt Luz's country home. The big home sat on about twenty acres of pine trees and was surrounded by a small golf course. A path went down to the stables where they had a few cows and a mean pale horse.

There were at least thirty people gathered around the tree after the nice meal. Laughter and conversation filled the room in competition with the clinking of glasses and squeals from the children. The fresh smell of the tree floated on the air. The fireplace's glow played with the lights of the tree as the family passed out the gifts.

From Luz to Ligia – my mom. Clapping and cheers went around the room.

Form Eduardo to Luz.

From so to so and so…

I stood in the back of the room waiting for my turn.

The room grew with animation, the room crowded with the rising cheers of cousins opening their presents, as a balloon being filled with hot air lifts high on the sky.

From Ligia to Jane… There, mother's gift for my sister.

I trembled with anticipation… *Mine is coming soon…I wonder what I am going to get…but, why is it taking so long? Where is my gift?*

From so to so.

The gifts under the tree were almost gone.

From so to so...

And they finished.

I stared at the empty bottom of the Christmas tree. Then I turned, opened the door and stepped out onto the terrace overlooking Medellín. I sat on the stairs and the city lights way down there sparkled on my tears.

Maybe I was adopted after all.

Life wasn't fair.

We lived in el barrio Los Angeles, a middle-class neighborhood. The neighbors across the street were big time cattle ranchers, and often invited me on weekends to their ranch about two hours from Medellín. We rode horses and worked with the cattle, vaccinating, branding, and counting them.

I made a few friends in the barrio, some were good influence, and some were not.

When I was about thirteen, one afternoon after school, *Luisito*, Little Louie, invited me to smoke marijuana. We were good friends. Sometimes we went to his country home in Caldas, a small town south of Medellín, where we fished, flew model airplanes, and ran around the pastures.

As we sat at the stairs of my apartment building he gave me the small pack of what appeared to be some kind of condiment.

I opened the package. "Humm, it smells good, sweet."

He handled me a piece of thin paper. "Here, make a cigarette with this…but I heard you have to take the seeds out."

I rolled it with difficulty, and lit it. I didn't feel any significant effect, but don't remember inhaling deeply. I'd had a bad experience with cigarettes.

I'd been caught smoking, so my father had me sit at the dining table and gave me a pack of *Piel Rojas*, his unfiltered cigarettes.

"Do you want to smoke? Here you go. Smoke them all." He sat across the table glaring.

After a few cigarettes, I bolted for the bathroom.

The irony was that he smoked two packs a day.

Nevertheless, smoking pot for the first time set a path for a cloudy future.

Life at home continued with its struggles. Mom barely made ends meet, and after a couple of years we had to move to a cheaper apartment downtown. It was housed in an older four-story building on top of a bar named *La Boa,* the python snake. I could tell it was hard for my mother, coming from a big wealthy family, to live in those conditions. I felt her bitterness and depression stream down her tears. She often sat in her bedroom and cried, cried, and cried. Sometimes my sister and I attempted to console her, but she just stared at the mirror and bawled.

I locked myself in my room and got stoned, but her high pitched wail came through the door anyway. *Why is my father living the good life while mom struggles like this? Life isn't fair…*

No, life wasn't fair, and to top it off, another dark cloud soon poured misery into my life.

When I was about fifteen, Gustavo, invited me to his apartment in Medellín, at a walking distance from my house. He served as my pilot role model and a figure of authority I trusted. At the apartment there were a few friends from his plantation. We drank and smoked pot. After a couple of beers I felt dizzy, like floating. I'd drunk beer with my dad at the plantation before, and now wondered why my vision blurred with only a few. I mentioned I wasn't feeling well, so Gustavo led me to a bedroom, and laid me on the bed. I saw someone else in the back of the room, a man who might have been his driver. It felt like a bad dream, and in the fog, under the cover of darkness, it happened. My body felt what my mind rejected. I was confused. I experienced an ugly pleasure that brought a corrupted future. Innocence was marred by spreading darkness, and trust was lost in its devastating wake.

The next day while walking home, I felt sad and dirty, confused and betrayed. A thousand questions rang through my head. *Why had this happened to me? Is this normal? Am I now part of a secret society? That wasn't supposed to happen between men. Why did my body feel like that? Is perversion part of success? Am I supposed to accept it and go with it?*

Regardless, it wasn't normal to me. Women attracted me. I had lost my virginity when I was fourteen, and thought about sex all the time, but, now, confused and my sexual identity compromised, sex took a twist. The seed of anger and bitterness sprang a tree of rotten fruit. I hated attracting men.

Gustavo never mentioned that night. He came around the plantation house when my dad wasn't there, harassing me continually. One time a plantation's worker saw him grabbing me. I hit him, and pleaded for him to stop and leave me alone, but he was big and strongly built. And now, other people knew

I felt powerless and trapped.

Feelings of distrust, emptiness, despair and depression, like the soldiers hidden inside the Trojan Horse of Greek mythology, tormented my mind and were dimmed, only temporarily, by drugs and alcohol.

3 THE ENEMY WITHIN

Months passed and I made new friends around La Boa. They were into prescription drugs, mushrooms, acid, and cocaine. I frequented bars and discos, met shady characters, smoked pot every day, and got drunk every weekend. My life became a psychedelic journey of rainbows and clouds, green fields and flowers, tears and pain. My outbursts of anger felt like thunder and lightening inside my brain and drugs became my hiding place.

Francisco, an attorney living across the street invited me to smoke pot and drink. He continued what Gustavo had started. He also invited my friends to orgies at high-class whore houses. My sex life was out of control, my identity confused, and drug use skyrocketed. Money and twisted sex seemed to go hand in hand.

My life swirled towards the drain with no hope insight.

At seventeen years old, wild, bitter, and high most of the time, my school performance was terrible. I had been a pretty good student, but now, because of my absences at the Conrado Gonzalez High School, I was expelled. Then, I enrolled in the San Juan Eudes High School on the hills South of Medellín and by now I smoked a joint, took a pill, and did a line of cocaine before getting on the school bus. When I got to school, I was flying high.

My grades continued failing until I got on probation. I cursed all the time, and carried a steel bar from the steering system of a car, my version of steel knuckles. It made me feel really tough and dangerous. I wanted to crush someone's face with it. Next, I purchased a small revolver, a six-shot Colt .32, but I only had four bullets and didn't have connections to buy more. Besides, it was in such bad condition that it probably would fall apart if fired.

The school's country setting was perfect for getting high. I smoked pot by the soccer field, and before the recess ended, did a line of cocaine, or took a pill, depending on the mood, sometimes both.

One day, in chemistry class my disturbance caused the teacher to stop the session and insisted I leave. That meant I'd failed four classes and would have to repeat it all. I yelled, insulted, and challenged him to a fight. Pulled out my brass knuckles and I got ready to charge. Everyone's eyes on me, embarrassed and confused, angry and defeated, I stormed out of the classroom.

The teacher summoned a special meeting with the principal and all the teachers. It didn't help that the Algebra and Philosophy teachers were his brothers. The school-day came to a halt. The principal called my mother. She came and they offered a deal. I was to leave the school voluntarily instead of being expelled. The conditions were not to retaliate against the chemistry teacher, and to never come near the school.

A few days later, I pulled my gun on the maid and threatened to kill her because she'd burnt my favorite shirt. Rage flowed through my veins when I saw that my tailored-made midnight blue satin shirt had an iron stamped in the middle of the back.

That outburst was the final straw. My party style was gone, and so was I. My mom had it. She called my father as I listened from my room.

"Hello Jack...I can't control him anymore. El Mono is going crazy..."

"You have to come and pick him up." She hung up and came into my room. "Pack, your dad is coming to pick you up."

***

It won't be that bad. After all, Dad had better cars and an apartment in El Poblado, a much nicer area of town.

I packed my dark green suitcase and waited. Emptiness overwhelmed me, turmoil and chaos whirled in my mind, feelings I was to become familiar with, an empty heart and an empty soul, living the empty life of the unwanted.

All these feelings pooling inside like a Trojan horse, like a virus waiting to be unleashed, emptiness and rage, bitterness and hate, and I saw no sunshine in the horizon, no hope in the future, only darkness.

My father pulled up and honked in the usual way. I came down and got in his car. He didn't say a word. A bad sign, I expected him to scream, hit me, something.

His apartment complex consisted of about ten four-stories buildings. His top-floor unit overlooked the pool. Standing at the window, I watched families having fun in the water. There were a lot of kids my age laughing and playing. But I felt out of place. At mom's home, she, my sister, and I, were nearly strangers, or at least that's how it felt to me. Seeing families—normal families—together, looked unreal. Nevertheless, I got ready to live the dream, to have a family life again.

The next morning my perspective changed. Dad woke me up. "Get ready. You're going to the plantation." He closed the door.

Well, good morning to you too, Dad...

He shipped me to Apartadó, a small town northwest of Medellín. The foreman picked me up at the airfield and took me to the plantation.

My father split his time between the plantation and in Medellín with his family. Away from the drug scene I cleaned up a little. Only smoked pot and drank. I even got drunk with my father after shipping days. Sometimes we argued, sometimes we were *buddies,* sometimes we went to whore houses together.

He also taught me to work on cars. He knew how to rebuild engines, do body-work, and paint. We overhauled the farm's trucks and a Jeep Commando he'd got for me. Each project took a long time, but they looked better than new when finished. If he didn't know something, he'd read the manual, and tried until he'd get it right. I learned about every part of those machines, every system. I handled the parts, drained the fluids, tighten the screws, and scraped my knuckles in the process.

These times with my dad helped me to discover one of my gifts. I understood systems and their purpose in any equipment I came to use. I even thought to have ESP, or some kind of special connection with engines.

One night I arrived at the plantation's house, parked in the garage, and walked to the building housing the electric generator. It was powered by an old Lister diesel engine that needed repairs and had several oil leaks. I propped my flashlight on an oil can and started to crank the engine. After gaining enough momentum, I released the valves to get it to start. It revved up a little, and then it died. I repeated the process with the same result. Then, I cranked it with all my might and released the valves again, but this time I put my hand over the engine, closed my eyes, and "willed" it to start. It gained speed, so I took my hand off and it started to die again. I put my hand over it, and gained speed, but only when I "willed" it to. It was weird, but it worked, the engine started. I could feel every part of that engine doing what it was supposed to do.

After that I could visualize every part, doing its purpose or failing, inside any machine I drove, rode, and eventually flew. I felt as a part of the machine.

Machines were trustworthy, and when well taken care of, appeared somehow grateful.

As a child, my father used to take me to Guaymaral airport near Bogotá. While he took flying classes, I stood with my nose against the window as he did touch and goes, landed and took off. A few times he walked me out to the ramp, and showed me the small plane, the controls, the engine, the smooth wings, and even taught me to drain the water from the gas tanks. He explained the function of the parts and systems of the aircraft. I loved the smell of gasoline, the heat of the tarmac, the roar of the planes, all about those beautiful machines. After he got his license he took me up a few times. I took pride in the fact that my dad was a pilot, even though he didn't fly much afterwards.

The raw power of the engines, the propeller unyielding path, the unnatural feeling of flying, combined with my fear of heights, gave me a rush, a cold feeling down my spine, and ignited a fire in my heart.

This beautiful feeling increased later by the helicopter rides I got from Ricardo, one of the pilots that flew the crop-dusters. He'd prank dad by zooming over us and releasing the yellowish residue of the chemical tanks over the truck while we drove unaware. Then, he'd land on the road and take me up. It was exhilarating. The roar of the engine, the smell of gas and chemicals, the vibration of the cold aluminum seat, the wind coming through the door-less cabin, the rotor blades' thundering, and seeing the people way down there through the Plexiglas bubble, it all moved the deepest parts of my soul. The only thing holding me from the void was the seatbelt.

I also had my share of involvement with private planes with Gustavo. He flew a twin-engine Piper Aztec and usually did a flyby over our house to signal my father to pick him up at the nearby private airfield. He'd overpass a couple of times, until he spotted us from the plane, and confirmed it by moving the wings' tips up and down. Dad and I waved back, jumped in the car, and raced towards the field. By the time we got there Gustavo had landed and unloaded the plane already inside the hangar. Sometimes he took us for a ride, and we even flew to Bogotá a couple of times. Gustavo was a good influence in my life, but also did great damage to my soul, and he bought my silence with a motorcycle.

Riding that motorcycle I had a horrible accident while running errands for the plantation. A truck cut on front of me to get in a gas station. I felt the rear tire slide and then darkness. My head hit against the steel step for the driver to get up to the cab. I fractured two vertebrae in my neck and was airlifted to Medellín, even though the town's hospital doctor told my father I wouldn't make it. On that flight to Medellín, I vowed to become a pilot.

Almost becoming a paraplegic didn't change my attitude. My rage became a desire to recuperate. It took me four months, and after the miracle, my rocky road continued.

I arrived back to the plantation and resumed my

responsibilities but things had changed. My father spent more time in Medellín where he was in the process of building a big house. At the same time, the plantation required more attention as production lowered. To increase production required re-planting another variety of trees that were shorter, allowing more plants per acre, and produced more bananas per bunch. This new variety required deeper drainage, which was costly to excavate, so Dad got a loan, but most of the money went to the construction of the house.

The plantation's truck driver told me that the foreman had been stealing fertilizer. I relayed the information to my father, but he didn't believe me. The foreman had informed him of my pot-smoking, which was true, but it made my discovery sound like a comeback.

The fertilizer showed on the plants as a fine white powder on the stem of the leaf, and one the sought effects was more weight of the fruit. A decreased amount of fertilizer still produced the fine powder, but not the desired weight. When my father finally believed me and figured that the ratio of bananas per box was too high, it was too late. The fertilizer was gone and so was the foreman.

The money problems increased and facing the workers when their check bounced was one duty I didn't want. Banks cancelled accounts and merchants recognized my signature. Changing banks and signatures didn't help. I still had to come home and face angry workers.

The plantations' jobs were brutal, and some of the workers were violent criminals running from the law. These titans fought constantly over women and drinks. I often transported stabbed workers to the hospital on the bed of the pick-up truck, or corpses chopped by machete to the morgue. Memories branded my young mind forever, haunting me on dark nights while driving back home.

One payday I came home finding a mob holding machetes and demanding their pay in cash. I told them I had to go to the bank to get the money.

Instead, I went to call my dad in Medellín through the Telecom office. The place was crowded, hot, and smelled of sweat. I gave the number to the operator and waited my turn. Then, after almost an hour, I heard my number called and went into the cabin. I cleaned the greasy headset with the corner of my shirt but couldn't get rid of the stomach-turning smell. I told dad about the workers, and the need to wire some money to cover the weeks' payroll. He went nuts, yelled that he had no money, and hung up. I pictured him enjoying the luxurious new home and living the big life.

I needed him to take his place and provide a solution, wire the money, do something, NOW. But instead, I saw doom galloping my way not too far off.

What should I do? Were the workers still waiting for me back home?

I climbed in the pick-up truck and cried on the drive home. When I got back to the plantation, relieved that the workers had gone back to their barracks, went into the house and toward my room. Anita, the eighty-year old cook, saw me pass by the kitchen's door and asked if I wanted some lentils soup, my favorite dish. I continued into my room without answering, sat on the bed, and bawling pulled my father's revolver out of my handbag. A bullet seemed like a good solution.

I looked at the big weapon—the black polished metal, the stained wood handle, the smell of oil, and the long, thick barrel staring silently back. Inside the cylinder, I could see the tips of the dum-dum bullets designed to expand on impact.

I was not a good son. But, regardless of my behavior and shortcomings, I didn't deserve this. I felt defrauded, abandoned and cornered.

Lifting the gun, I felt the cold metal against my temple, as if someone else held it, as if my arm and my head were not connected anymore. *What reason do I have for living?*

Shaking, I shot the wall. I was not going to quit, no matter what. I didn't need this. Alone, discarded, and broken...but not a quitter, a failure, or worthless. A broken soul in a thickening iron cast.

Anita raced into my room, and sat quietly on the bed by my side, her small and thin frame slouching.

This wasn't fair. Holding the smoking gun, I felt cheated, bitter, and unjustly punished. I hated my father with all my heart.

The fall didn't take long, after trying to keep the plantation afloat for a while, my father sold it.

I returned to Medellín, lived at my father's apartment in El Poblado and worked as a waiter at a popular pizzeria. One night at work, a breathtaking brunette came in with Alvaro a new friend that lived across the street from the restaurant. He introduced us.

Mary Ann, broken hearted by a musician gone to America, captivated my mind and heart. My mission became to help her forget and heal. She taught me to make batik, the art of dyeing cloth with a wax-resist technique. We smoke pot and worked on her studio at the back of her father's mansion.

I came up with the idea of opening a restaurant and told my

father. Mary Ann, my father, and I became partners. We rented and remodeled an old house, and in the back built a mezzanine where I lived.

The business picked up, we sold steaks, lasagna, and pizza. My dad's cooking abilities translated into customer satisfaction and profits. My previous experience as a disc jockey at one of the small town's clubs in the plantation area entertained the clientele after dinner. Shortly after my taste for cocaine opened a new venture and I sold small quantities to support my habit.

Some nights we, Mary Ann and I, handled the bar, played good music and had a good time together. On the days off, we smoked pot, did art, went on road trips and partied. Her family *accepted* me, but our fights increased and became a bit notorious. One time, we argued at her house and she climbed onto the hood of my car trying to stop me from leaving. I drove down to the plaza of El Poblado, about a quarter of a mile, with her holding onto the hood. People stared while I waited for the stop light to change. I just looked forward.

I drove around the plaza and back to her house. I rang the bell and her dad came out. He was a gentle giant. I can still see his pleasant and wise face as he looked at her precious youngest daughter, calmly convincing her that it was better for her to get off of the car, and into the house.

After about a year, Mary Ann decided to step out of the partnership and my father bought her share of the business.

My drug use and dad's drinking collided one night after closing.

I'd served him a rum and coke, and he slurred, "Why don't you go back with Gustavo?"

"What do you mean...?" I blinked, not sure if I'd misunderstood. I couldn't believe my ears. "You...you knew?" I stammered. "You should have intervened..." My brain boiled as fire surged from the pit of my stomach.

"All you do well is party...you went there..." He slurred.

"I can't believe it. Why you didn't even mentioned it...you should have protected me."

He threw his drink on my face.

"I am out of here." I walked out from behind the bar and walked towards the front door but he stepped on front of me.

"You're not going anywhere..." He advanced towards me.

"Get out of my way." I cursed him.

He blocked my way out and took a swing.

Tired of a life of abuse, I stepped back avoiding his blow, and took one of my own. He fell down. I looked at him sprawled on the floor. He wouldn't get up. Then he moved, and slowly got up. I left the restaurant and went to one of my hang outs up in the mountains by the El Retiro dam. A beautiful lake surrounded by forest. The next day I came back to find the front-door's lock changed, and one of my workers telling me through the window that I wasn't allowed in, "Just following orders".

I stepped away from the door to face a cloudy and uncertain future.

4 THE SOUL FOR SALE

Alvaro, my new friend, spoke to his family and they took me in for a while. After that, I lived with friends and moved from house to house.

My uncle intervened and I got a settlement from my share of the restaurant, with it I bought Italian jewelry smuggled from Panama. Later on, my mother told me about an art school near her house that had a jewelry fabrication class. I enrolled and began making custom pieces. JRausch Jewelry my first business on my own, my lifetime hobby, and cover for my later criminal enterprises, was born. I worked as a jeweler for anyone who cared to ask.

Making decent money, I pursued my dream of becoming a pilot. The Colombian Air Force wouldn't accept me because my nearsightedness fell above the degree allowed by the guidelines, which also prevented me from flying for Commercial Airlines. Nevertheless, I attended flight school and obtained my Private Pilot License.

Learning to fly took me through magnificent experiences. I flew solo for the first time in a small airfield near Santa Fe de Antioquia, west of Medellín, in November 27th, 1981. At 23 years of age, wild, adventurous, and eager to make my own life choices, that first flight marked my adult life with a real accomplishment.

The instructor flew with me from Medellín, we practiced "touch-and-goes" - landings and take offs- for a while. Then he told me to stop after the next landing. I didn't question him, just did what he'd said.

I taxied to the ramp and parked. He opened the door and told me, "Go ahead, you are ready to solo." He stepped on the wing, got off, and closed the door.

My heart thumped so hard I could hear it on the headsets. I looked at him standing by the tip of the wing and nodded. He gave me the thumbs up. I looked forward, then back at him, and I nodded again. He waved me forward. I let go of the brakes, applied power and the plane slowly rolled forward. When the single engine Piper PA-28 got to the runway, I looked both ways before entering it, taxied to the end, and turned facing my destiny.

Stepping on both brakes – each pedal controls a wing's wheel – I applied full power. The little plane, a marvelous machine to me, shook and screamed. I let go of the brakes. It rolled slowly first, then picked up enough speed to rotate -pulled the wheel- the front tire lifted, and then the wings'. I was airborne, flying solo for the first time.

I retracted the flaps, climbed to the assigned altitude, and reduced power. Then, I followed the pattern around the airfield reporting on the radio my intentions in case some other trainer or visitor joined my adventure. I did my three official touch-and-goes and stopped. My face hurting from grinning, chest forward and feeling taller, I stepped off the plane to receive the congratulations of my instructor.

A couple of days later, the entire academy's students took a two day trip to Santagueda, a runway about an hour south of Medellín. I flew with the instructor and on approach to land he said, "There is a little crosswind, be careful later, it may pick up." I nodded and finished landing. We practiced for a while, and again, he told me to stop, got off, and waved me to go. The next forty minutes of pure flying-heaven made me feel complete and confident. The instructor called me from another plane -the airfield had no control tower- told me to "Put it down."

When I got off the plane, there was a mob of students waiting to give me my official "Solo Ceremony." One chopped chunks of my mane –Trasquilado- then another poured used motor oil on my head. To finalize, I was handed a big glass of Aguardiente -a strong drink made of sugar cane- to drink it all. The adrenaline rush and the effect of the Aguardiente made my head spin. The instructor gave me the airplane's keys. "Tomorrow you are on your own." All congratulated, patted my back, and joked as I stumbled to the strip's hotel.

The next day, I got up at the crack of down, showered, got ready, and walked to the airfield. The feeling of freedom and power gave me a rush as I walked on the grass path towards the ramp. The cold weather didn't bother me, and as the sun appeared on the horizon, I felt as born again. A new life spread on front of me, and a sky of limitless opportunities opened up.

I performed the pre-flight check and got in the cockpit. I didn't feel any wind. The engine cranked to life and the blue machine shook. After warming the engine, and all ready to go, I released the parking brake and taxied to the end of the runway. By now other students were following the same procedure around the field.

I stepped on the brakes, applied full power, and ran down the runway getting me airborne, nothing new, or out of the ordinary so far. It looked like a beautiful day to fly. I went around the pattern without a problem until I turned into the final approach.

As I got close to the field, and descended to land, a gusty crosswind pushed the plane out of the landing path. I had to abort the landing and go around. I had never experienced a crosswind that strong, ever. I had heard stories about flying the plane against the crosswind sideways until about to touch the ground, then, straightened and aligned, made a safe landing. But, I had never done it or experienced with an instructor. Instructors can't produce those flight conditions.

I went around and tried again. Concentrating, and grabbing the wheel with all my might, I tried to compensate for the wind by pushing the left pedal activating the rudder. Oh, what a deadly dance, it wasn't fair. Strong gusts hit the plane, and as I compensated or overcompensated trying to put it down, the flight path seemed to drift to my left. Now I was really low, almost on the ground, and as the plane drifted off the path, I applied full power again. Almost hitting the fence that bordered the field, farm workers jumped on the ground as I zoomed over them.

By now, the other students had stopped their preflight inspections, and an instructor yelled on the radio, "Rausch put it down. Put it down however you can, and I'll give you more double-command"

That made me mad.

"What do you think I am trying to do?" I yelled and slammed the mike on the holder.

"Just put it down...I know you can do it..." He said unconvincingly.

What am I going to do? Mental block, I had no solutions. I didn't cross my mind to go to another airport nearby, or fly back to Medellín, or…Well, there were no options at the moment. I had to land no matter what.

I continued the pattern reciting, "Velocidad y altura, te libra de la sepultura. Velocidad y altura, te libra de la sepultura." – Speed and altitud, save me from the sepulcher.

As I turned into the final approach, I recited softly, and determined to fight the gusts I grabbed the wheel and started the pedal dance. Pressing the left pedal gave the plane an angle to face the wind and compensate the drift. I reduced power and felt the plane sink, and drift, so I gave it a little power and rudder. The gusts hit the left side without mercy. Now I was flying too fast and the plane floated, and floated. Passing the runway threshold and continued fighting the gusts. Finally I put the plane down and I had more than half of the runway to go. To prove I could do it, I applied power and tried to take off. The radio crackled.

"Rausch stop now." The instructor yelled.

I could see the ramp and the two parked planes on my right. A few students stood by looking at my plane approach screaming down the runway.

"There is not enough runway for take off Rausch, stop, stop now."

I looked at the speed gauge and calculated…The speed to lift could not be reached before the fence. The strip sloped down a little at the end…and by now, I had not enough strip to stop either. I remembered a trick a pilot friend of mine had told me. The flaps on the wings are panels on the rear edge, that when lowered, improve lift at slower speeds. So I retracted the flaps to clean the plane's profile and help it gain the few knots of airspeed. Right before hitting the fence I applied full flaps, and the plane, with the extra lift, jumped and cleared the fence. Beep, beep, beep, the stall alarm went on. I was going to crash. The mountain sloped down, so I lowered the nose and acquired those precious miles per hour needed to fly safely and climb. The radio was silent.

I went around and continued doing the touch-and-goes. Each time I landed better, cleaner. The instructor didn't call on the radio again, but had much to say when I finished.

In my new life, unseen danger lurked at every corner, but my desire to succeed was stronger.

After graduating and receiving my license I was invited to "check an airfield." An acquaintance from the airport wanted to show me a route. This was the opportunity I had been looking for, so I went home to celebrate my license and the invitation.

That night I drank beer, and stared at my license in awe. I couldn't sleep, and when I finally went to sleep it was late. I had to be at the airport at 6 a.m. but I got there at 6:15. He was gone, and never invited me again.

My dream became to do a flight to the US for the cartel. It was not an easy branch to get into, and once in, it was not an easy one to get out of. The quickest way out, and the most common, was the grave. I didn't care. My soul was for sale.

While in flight school I had been house-sitting for a friend, and as in most nice buildings in Medellín, there lived a Mafioso, Gil. I knew one of his soldiers.

One day as I parked my car, he drove into the garage in his black Porsche followed by a Toyota Land Cruiser full of bodyguards. I timed it and met them at the stairs. My acquaintance introduced us, and I took my shot offering my services as a pilot. I had done my homework and knew he owned a Cessna 210

Centurion, a remarkable single engine plane. I would do anything to get that job.

He agreed to give me a try. I began as a co-pilot on a flight to Bogotá. We met at the Olaya Herrera, Medellín's Municipal Airport, and as we were doing the airplane's preflight inspection, I froze, a Lear Jet taxied by. It was one of the few private business jets at that airport. A notorious mafia family of that time, the Ochoas, had a Falcon. And the Lear taxiing by was Pablo Escobar's, the most violent mafia boss of the era. My pulse soared and a cold knot filled my stomach. I hid behind my sunglasses. I wanted to fly one of those, but I tried to make my staring not too obvious. *El Doctor* was in town.

Gil's pilot was a new hire also. The flight went without problems until we neared the canyon coming into Bogotá. Clouds covered the left mountain, so when he asked me which side to take, I thought he was kidding, a trick question. Still, I suggested the clear side.

He flew into the clouds and panicked. He asked me what to do, and I was so upset I wanted to drop him. There was a passenger on the back of the plane, and heard us arguing, he could see the same, nothing. It was like swimming in milk, a thick white curtain waiting to open for the last scene of our lives, splattered on the steep face of the mountain. I glanced back. He was as white as the clouds. Welcome to Cartel-Air.

I was too angry to be afraid, but then, I knew this crew was not going to stick together long. There was nothing to do but wait for impact. Flying at 190 miles per hour there was no time to say "Jesus" if the face of the mountain appeared. Instead, the sunshine and the open fields of the high plateau surrounding the city appeared, and I breathed again.

We landed in Bogotá, went to a hotel, and waited for the plane to come back from a flight with another crew, but it never did. That plane disappeared.

Gil arrived in Bogotá the next day and we partied until he sent me back to Medellín driving one of his cars. It's easy to entice a soul for sale, and he seemed to know my price. I was twenty four years old in a brand new BMW. Machines with big engines paved a quick way to my heart.

I ran errands for Gil, drove women to his ranch, took his mom to the bank, and even transported a horse from Bogotá to Medellín, in a small truck. The horse might have been injected with a drug. It kicked the walls of the truck if anyone got close. It prevented the check-points' police from searching the saddle box, most likely about 300 kilos. That's what we called a *gancho ciego,* a blind-hook. They didn't tell me what I was carrying and I didn't ask. This was my initiation. Later, I became the driver and bodyguard for Gil's mom.

Now I became one of the guys driving Toyota Land Cruisers, BMWs and Porsches. I was a *Mágico,* a magician, the common name for Mafioso, coming up with a bunch of things out of nothing. Nobody knows the price to get involved.

Gil's mom was a tough woman, lots of yelling and lots of idiosyncrasies, everything had to be done her way, on her time, and to her pleasing. Nothing made her happy. After two years of working for her, I told Gil I couldn't take it any longer. I wanted to get involved in the business, make real money. I was taking high risks. He called it "work for points", it didn't jive with me, and I didn't care for points. I wanted money. He told me to quit working for his mom and then he would bring me back into the crew.

I quit and went back to help my father at the pizzeria. My

uncle had interceded and we were back in good terms.

Another connection got me the job at the *Runway to Hell*. We loaded cocaine going out, and unloaded contraband coming in. Those action-packed operations paid well, but I wanted to fly.

I was connected, but I didn't value the opportunities. Envy and greed were my perpetual non-paying passengers. Blinded, I overlooked the avenues towards my goal. Money and women dimmed my passion to fly.

I ran into Gil again and asked him for work. He offered me a job in Miami, and without much thought, I said, yes.

He sent me to Bogotá, where the U.S. Embassy was located. I applied for a tourist visa, and in about a week, all the paperwork was done.

All the while, partying with the boss and his partner presented an angle to the mafia scene I wasn't prepared for. Some people sought to advance by gossiping and back-stabbing. It played like a bad soap opera where everyone was armed, lazy, and stupid, and some drop-dead gorgeous.

After obtaining the visa, Gil sent me to Medellín in another Porsche. Young, crazy, and feeling connected, I drove like Fittipaldi on crack, but didn't need the racetrack. No wonder people paid for that kind of technology. What a rush.

My orders were to take care of everything the car needed, then to park it at his spot at the building's garage. No problemo, sweet deal. *If you want, I can wear out the tires so you get new ones too.*

I arrived late at night to Medellín and got up next day ready to *fix* the Porsche. Got it washed, installed new windshield wipers, changed the oil, and in the process drove it all over town.

My father and I had dinner at the pizzeria. He joked about the car, and then he said. "I am proud of you, Mono."

I looked at him. A feeling of emptiness overwhelmed me. *Was he kidding? Being sarcastic?* He was serious. How sad, proud of me being a criminal.

Anger and bitterness overwhelmed me. *Don't you remember that night when you shouted that you knew Gustavo had raped me....you, blamed me. Did he rape you too? What dark secret you hold my sick alcoholic father?*

I looked into his pale blue eyes and remembered his bragging about the orgies with Gustavo and his wife, about the accountant's wife...*you made me sick. You destroyed my mom's life...*

As we finished dinner and had drinks, the three brothers of Gil's partner came in. They were hefty guys. The older one said. "We have been trying to catch you all day. You drive like a mad man." His brothers stood behind.

I stood. "How are you doing? Want a drink something?" I waved towards the bar.

He stepped forward. "Gil said to give us the car's keys."

I sat down again. "Gil told *me* to get it ready, and park it at *his* apartment. And that is what I am going to do."

He turned, looked at his brothers, and they looked at each other. "Okay, then. I will report that to Gil."

I waved them off. "Do that."

He stormed out with his troop behind.

I looked at dad. "That was not fun."

He shrugged. I hated when he did that. He looked defeated and hopeless.

One of the partner's brothers was also a pilot. He had heart problems and suffered black-outs. He'd told me in a party. I looked at him expecting to laugh but he wasn't joking. The competition was crazy, and mafia politics were worse than I expected.

Gil traveled to Medellín a couple of days later. So, I came to his apartment to give him some details of the trip.

Levy, my acquaintance, opened the door. "Hey Jako, come in, come in…" He swayed.

The sweet smell of smoked cocaine hung in the air like a stormy cloud. Gil went on smoking binges for days.

Levy led me downstairs. Two other guys I had seen before at the office drank beer and chatted. They nodded. I nodded back.

"Where is Gil?"

"He's in the bedroom…busy…" Levy winked. "It's gonna be a long night." He handed me a beer.

I sat down and took a swig.

The apartment had three levels. The dining room and kitchen were on the entrance level, two bedrooms upstairs, and downstairs, separated by the stairs to the upper level, were the master bedroom, and to the other side the living room, where we sat.

A couple of hours later, as I went to the kitchen to get more beer, I heard the door of Gil's bedroom open. A woman came up the stairs. She was the wife of an acquaintance of mine from the plantation area. She looked down, went to the front door and out.

My stomach turned. *That wasn't right...Why would she do that?*

I looked at Levy. He shrugged. We knew her husband. He was one of those guys that had their hand in all the pots. Now, Gil had *his* in his pot.

My morals were not up to a high standard, but seeing a powerful man entice someone's wife to drugs and sex made me sick.

Gil came out of his cave, charm dripping on the floor.

We made plans to meet in Miami in a few weeks. His travels were surrounded by mystery, like the devil, he suddenly appeared everywhere.

He didn't even mention the incident with the Porsche. He had two. I liked the black one better but nobody drove it but him.

When I got to Miami, Gil took me to his home. He owned an *Import and Export* business. It seemed like everyone operated the same type of business. I hung out with him at the office, sat outside of meetings, and fetched espressos. I was a coffee-runner-bodyguard with no gun.

The routine was broken by a trip to a kennel. We took a twin-engine plane to a private runway in the middle of the state. The owner of the ranch drove us to the property. The dog's demonstration impressed us. It attacked the heavy padded worker with zeal. There kennels held beautiful dogs of all breeds, colors, and sizes, but Gil wanted *the dog*. The humongous German shepherd was gorgeous. The owner of the ranch reluctantly parted with his best friend for $10,000 dollars.

After about a month of Florida's sunshine, Gil told me that the office handling the distribution in California had become available.

That meant that the person in charge had been arrested. I didn't think twice about the implications of coming into the hot spot.

5 THE PROMISED LAND

This was the opportunity I had been waiting for. The terms were handling everything for a certain amount per kilo, or half of that if he paid the costs of operation. I figured that the full amount would give me more autonomy, money, and power.

Miguel, a guy from the office, bought my plane ticket under another name. I had no idea, until I got to the airport. At the check-in counter I was requested my identification, and when I showed her my Colombian passport, the lady loudly asked why my ticket was under another name. On top of that, I had the flu, sweat ran down my face, and wore a sport jacket to dim the chills. I told her the truth, that the person at the office had made a mistake. Truth had gotten me out of trouble before, but she still made me pay for another ticket, which left me only $200 for the trip.

As I walked towards the boarding gate, two DEA agents approached. They flashed their badges, "Identification please."

"Sure." I handed him my passport, as a block of ice build in my stomach.

An airline's baggage handler brought my suitcase.

"Do we have your permission to search your suitcase? *This is* your suitcase, isn't it?" He pointed at the green suitcase with my passport.

"Yes. That is mine. Go ahead."

One agent dived into the suitcase with gusto, as the other continued questioning me.

"Welcome to the U.S. *Jack.*" His voice dripped with sarcasm. "How did you come up with that name? What are you going to do in California?"

After explaining my German ancestry, I made a story about going to visit a friend that owed me money. Lies and truth streamed calmly. I had done some modeling for jeans, brandy, and soft drinks, but I didn't know my acting potential until then.

The agent searching the suitcase closed it and got up.

They looked disappointed, wished me a good trip, and went away.

Gil and his girlfriend, a striking olive-skinned brunette -not the *wife* from the house- had driven me to the airport, but had stealthily moved away until the DEA agents left. They joined me later and Gil made no mention of the ticket switch or of the search.

After the plane took off, I realized that in the confusion Gil had not given me the number of my contact in California. He might have done it on purpose, but it turned out for the best.

At Los Angeles airport, two DEA agents waited for me outside the door of the plane. "Welcome to California *Jack.* Please come with us." He held his badge two inches from my nose.

They escorted me out of the boarding gate, and as we

entered the building another agent trailed behind.

"Let's get you luggage." My entourage stormed into the baggage claim area and we waited for my suitcase to come around the carrousel. I spotted it and they grabbed it, put it on the floor, and dove in.

A woman in a mink coat stared with drawn eyebrows while her limousine driver got her luggage. I shrugged and shot her a flirty smile. I wished she waited for me...my vivid imagination traveled at the speed of sound. The distraction helped me to remain calm.

The agent in charge was less friendly than the one in Florida.

"What brings you here Mr. Rausch?"

"Vacation."

"How much money are you bringing?" His eyes lit up.

"Two hundred dollars, there was a mistake in Florida and I had to purchase another ticket."

"What are you going to do with two hundred dollars, go to the Olympics?"

He didn't ask about the problem with the ticket, so I knew he had the information I had given the agents in Miami. I expected the 1984 Olympic Games to heighten security, and this much attention gave me a rush.

Their still-hunt turned me into a chameleon.

"A friend totaled my car in Colombia, and is going to pay me back here." I was surprised at how convincing I sounded.

"Where is your friend?" He growled.

"I misplaced his number. I have to call my mother in Colombia to get it for me. Could you recommend a cheap hotel?"

The searching agent stood.

I looked at my clothes spilled on the floor, and then glared at him.

He shrugged, and showed coffee stained teeth.

"There is an information board right over there." The agent in charge pointed to the brightly lit hotel information board. He shoved the passport into my hand, turned around and left followed by his troop.

They disappeared into the crowd.

How long were they going to follow me? I walked to the information board and called a hotel.

The hotel van came and took me to a hole-in-the-wall near the airport. I watched TV and only left the room to get beer and chips from a nearby convenience store. After a couple of days, I called the office in Miami for my contact's number, and Rafa picked me up later that night.

Gil had offered the tienda to him also, but I didn't care. We stayed in a house he'd rented in Huntington Beach, watched TV, and went for rides. We got paid $200 a week for waiting. Gil came to visit and told me to rent a condo, then sent the other guy back to Florida.

My companion found himself used and dropped. He had worked in New York before, and I figured Gil wanted a fresh person in charge.

Something made me uneasy.

I leased a comfortable, two-bedroom condo in Garden Grove, furnished it, got a Volkswagen Jetta, and enrolled in the University of California English as a Second Language program. To everyone, I was an employee of a mining company.

Armed with a pager, I settled for the wait.

I loved the UCI program. The students were a mix of Middle Easterners, Asians, and a few South Americans, a good group, and nice teachers. It gave me a sense of normalcy. My favorite teacher was Mary, a beautiful Italian, nice and professional. I wished she hadn't been quite so professional.

About two months later, I got arrested for driving drunk in Huntington Beach. I forgot to turn on the headlights, drove half a block, and got pulled over. The officer came to my window and knocked. I didn't respond, so he opened the door and I fell out of the car. He helped me to his cruiser.

The DUI was expensive, and I spent a weekend in jail as part of the sentence.

I had been detained a few times in Colombia, twice for marijuana, and another for a bar fight, but was released after a couple of hours.

Mary drove me to the jail. I told her that if my boss at the mining company found out about my DUI, he'd fire me.

My college boy experience was short lived. The call to pick up the load came and I didn't want the exposure at the University anymore. The students always made comments about my pager going off, and Mary would say, "Colombia calling." If only she knew, maybe she could have talked me out of it.

But now there was no turning back.

A few months later, I saw Mary at a restaurant/disco in Irvine. She sat at a booth with an older gentleman.

"Hey, Maria. How are you doing?" I stood on front of their booth.

"Good Jack, how are you? We missed you." She smiled. "Thomas, this is Jack, one of my students." She said to her companion. "Jack, this is Thomas."

He squinted behind his wire-rimmed glasses. "Nice to meet you, Jack."

"Nice to meet you, Sir." I kept looking at her. She looked great.

"So, what you think? How do I look now?" I showed off my fancy clothing. I had a grey sport jacket, black silk shirt, linen slacks, and black alligator shoes. I loved alligator shoes and boots.

She looked me up and down, and said. "You look like a *Mafioso*."

My smile flew away. I was embarrassed, deflated. A feeling of emptiness grew within me. "It was good to see you Mary." I took a swig of my drink. "Nice to meet you, Thomas."

"Bye, Jack." They said in a chorus.

I blended into the background.

The loads came and I embraced the projects with gusto.

The roll came to me naturally. It absorbed me, and I thrived.

I made appointments in the morning, and delivered at lunch or dinner time. I met the clients, drove their car to the condo, loaded it, and left it back at the restaurant while they waited. It was easy money or at least, it appeared to be.

After the first operation, Gil sent Sam to work with me. I didn't know what kind of arrangement they had, nor did I care to ask.

Sam and I made a good team. He dressed well, spoke good English, and was popular with women, even though he missed his wife and young child back in Florida. We coordinated the deliveries, and learned to work together as we went.

We received 200 or 300 kilos, and delivered as little as 20. The lower the amount delivered, the closer that client was to the street dealers and the higher the risk.

I looked forward to delivering, and didn't take full advantage of Sam's participation. I met the clients, picked up the cars, loaded, and dropped them not too far from where the meeting had taken place. Almost the same procedures but now Sam was supposed to pick me up, and then I'd call the client and tell him where the loaded car was. We watched from a distance as the client got in the car, and then reported the delivery to the office in Florida.

An incident proved the system was flawed.

That morning I drove to a Mexican restaurant to meet a client. While I was waiting, two women came in and chose a table near the entrance. Seated at a higher level, by the veranda, I had good view of the entrance and of the lower level that was built as a little plaza, with a fountain in the middle surrounded by tables, and the salad bar to one side.

I noticed that after getting their food from the salad bar, the two women weren't interested in eating but in the people coming in and out of the place. In their mid-thirties, elegant but casual, big purses and low heeled-shoes, they blended well with the executive lunch crowd.

My contact was late and I felt restless. One of the women got up from the table, went to the salad bar again, and on the way to her table passed by the veranda near my table.

"Waiting for somebody?" Lots of perfect white teeth flashed.

"Yes, business. And you?" I flirted back.

"What do you do?"

"I design custom jewelry, and you?"

"Got a business card?" She pushed without answering.

"What do *you* do?" I forced a smile.

"Just out with my girlfriend, got to go, bye." She walked back to her table.

My stomach felt like a block of ice. *Should I call it off? That look in her appraising eyes...cold...Are they police?*

A guy came in, looked around, and we made eye contact. I nodded. We had swapped descriptions on the phone. He came to the upper level.

"Sergio?" I got up and pointed to the seat across from me.

"Yes. Are you Ricardo?" He said.

"Nice to meet you." I shook his hand, and sat down. "You

are late. I was about to leave." I sipped my drink.

"I don't know the area." He looked at the table.

I didn't ask where he came from. The least I knew, the better.

The waiter came and he ordered a soda.

He sat the car keys on the table. "It's a white Chevrolet parked to the right of the entrance."

"Did you bring a duplicate as I told you?" I placed my hand on top of the keys.

"Yeah." His eyes flashed anger.

The waiter came back with the soda. "Are you ready to order?"

"No. Give us a minute please." I said.

"I'll be back in a few minutes." The waiter walked away.

"Their carne asada is delicious. I'll page you my code when the car is back. I'll leave the keys in the ashtray, and lock it. You *do* have the duplicate, yes?" I took the keys, and got up holding his gaze.

"Yes." He looked annoyed.

"Enjoy your meal." I walked away, jaw clenched, the block of ice spreading from my stomach to the rest of the body.

I went to the bathroom and splashed some water on my face, got into one of the stalls and waited a while. Then, walked out to the parking lot, got in the car, and drove away. The ramp to the highway was around the corner, so I took it and drove south. Changing lanes carefully I merged in the fast lane and blended with the speed of traffic. Two cars had gotten in the freeway behind me, a small red one, and a grey four door sedan. After a few miles, I moved into the slower lanes. The grey sedan followed. She was two cars behind me. In my rearview mirror, I could see her dark hair though the windows of the car behind me. I changed to the right lane, and slowed down. She passed by me. I cut through the traffic getting out of the freeway, and took the ramp. I looked at her. She stared. I waved.

What I most feared had come upon me. *What am I going to do now? How many more are following?* I looked for the police helicopter, or a slow flying small plane, and drove around through the neighborhood I'd scouted days before as an escape route. Nobody suspicious followed.

I drove to a nearby mall and after parking the car across the street, I strolled over to one of the department stores, bought new clothing, changed, and went into the movie theaters. After calling Sam from the payphones, I waited for him inside the showroom. Darkness covered my fear.

The client paged me. I told him the delivery was cancelled.

"What do you mean? Where is the car?" He yelled.

"It's at the mall up the street from where you are."

"That is almost a mile walk."

"So, you *do* know the area." I hung up.

We abandoned the car I'd driven to the meeting, threw away the pager, and called Miami with the emergency code -911- and went home to regroup.

The rest of the week, we moved the load to another home, got extra pagers, and bought an extra car.

Safety became my obsession.

Paranoia, my common companion, left no space for friends. The line between good and evil faded. *Jack,* my old-self, got lost in the stormy sea of alcohol and blow, the enemy within gradually took over the ship.

A few days later, I went to the mail box center, the address I had on my driver's license and cars' registration. Along with bills and junk mail, I found a business card from a law enforcement agent. It had a piece of tape on the edge, and written instructions to call him with information. They were getting close.

I started using another identity which brought some relief, but made no difference if someone inside the organization had decided to give me up.

6 THE MONEY ROLLS

Business thrived, loads came and went. The amounts of cash passing through my hands clouded my sense of value. I filled the void buying whatever my heart desired. Drowning my fears and shortcomings made Dom Perignon, Jose Cuervo, and Margaritas my common companions. I had it all, but there was no satisfaction.

On Christmas time, the easy going manner of doing business showed another face. People got greedier. Some reported fewer kilos received, and others shortages with the payments I made. I kept my side of the organization tight. It was easy between me and Sam. He was honest and somehow naïve, or a very good actor. As a matter of fact, he had been a fashion model also, and had even auditioned for a movie.

The Florida crew wanted me out, though. A few times I took the hit, and had to take the loss. It was cheaper to pay than going to war. My standard was that killing for less than a million dollars was not worth it, and the rip offs never came to that.

Sam and I celebrated between operations, we frequented clubs in Newport Beach and attracted quality company. He missed his wife and son, and confided in me about his intimate secrets.

One night, dancing at a club, we met a reporter from Texas visiting her friend. We went to the house in Garden Grove and had a wonderful time. I saw the Texan once again but didn't realize how special this woman was, until I had tainted the relationship with cocaine. We went to the Ritz Carlton in Dana Point, ordered Dom Perignon, and I got too high…The next day I had to hire a taxi to take her to Los Angeles airport, never to see her again.

The dusty storms of white powder clouded my vision and diverted my path into the abyss.

Business continued with the usual shortcomings.

The shipments from Florida were coordinated by Miguel and Jose with Rafa as the driver. On one shipment they stole one kilo. They supposedly packed 38 kilos in the special compartment of the car, but I unpacked 37 with Rafa.

"Did you load the car with them?" I asked him.

"No, they loaded it."

I didn't read any hard feelings. Rafa said that transportation was more lucrative and not as slaving or risky as distribution.

Not wanting to loose my position over small details, I let that pass and paid for it. But when I sent $180,000 dollars, and they counted $143,000, that was different, it was straight out robbery.

Usually 100 bills of each denomination were bundled with a couple of rubber bands making easier to count. Yes, $37,000 was only a few bundles. 3 bundles of $100s, 1 of $50s, and 1 of $20s, but I wouldn't make that mistake. The cash fit perfectly inside the appliances, so nothing would shift inside the factory's box while shipping. I also removed a heavy part from the appliance to compensate for the weight of the cash. Everything was calculated perfectly, and re-packed flawlessly, down to the commercial size staples, and metal strap around the original box.

I flew to Florida to talk to Gil and it felt like walking into a lions' cave.

Jose picked me up at the airport.

"Hey, good to see you Jako." He said.

"Good to see you Jose." I forced a smile.

We walked out of the terminal, and as we drove out of the airport, I asked, "Jose, you counted the money with Miguel, right?" I looked at him.

"Yes, we counted together." He stared at the road.

"How much was missing?" I kept a conversational tone.

"$37,000"

"How much was missing on each of the packages?"

"I don't know. We unpacked it all, and then counted it." He looked at me and shrugged.

"So you don't know if the missing money came from one of the packages?"

"No, there was $143,000. That's what we counted."

It made sense to unpack and count, and he made it sound so believable, so I decided not to press, but, it nagged me. The money missing would have left a space in the packaging, or extra cash in my stash. That never happened to me.

We rode in silence for a while, until he drove into a warehouse.

"Gil is at home, he wants you to go there tomorrow morning." He got out of the car and I followed him into an empty office. Handing me a key, he said, "He wants you drive the Targa while in Miami." It's parked at front, he pointed to another door.

"Okay." I'll see you.

I grabbed my handbag and opened the door. The sight of the black Porsche gave me a rush.

"That?" I looked back at him.

"See you." He smiled, and strutted out into the warehouse.

Is he setting me up?

I got my handbag, threw it on the passenger's seat, and drove to a Hilton nearby. Somehow even the pleasure of driving that gorgeous machine was gone.

I didn't sleep well. On the forty-five minute drive to Gil's house my stomach twisted. Accusing his crew of stealing was a bad move, but if I didn't, it would appear as if I was the one with the accounting problems. Neither the German engineering, nor the gorgeous Florida sunshine calmed the sour churning in my stomach. *Gil's trust is going to be lost if I don't handle the meeting well. How can I turn this to my advantage?*

I finally made it to his house and his wife opened the door. "Hi Jako, come in, it's good to see you." She led me to the living room.

"Good to see you too." I had driven her a couple of times to Gil's huge cattle ranch in Colombia.

"Make yourself comfortable, he'll be right out." She waved me into a plush couch, and walked away.

"Thanks." I stood looking out the window into the manicured lawn and the lake behind it. Breathing slowly to try to clam my racing heart, sweat run down my back, and my face felt cold and clammy.

"Hey Jako, let's have breakfast." Gil passed by toward the dinning room, and I followed.

I was not hungry but refusing would start the meeting with the wrong foot.

"Good to see you boss."

"Sit there." He pointed to the chair to his left.

Facing the wall left my back open to the house and didn't make me feel better. *They wouldn't kill me in his house...Would they?*

The dining table contained enough food for a dozen. The aroma of scrambled eggs, bacon, sausage, toast, and coffee, almost made me hungry.

He served himself and pointed with the knife. "Dig in Jako. A full stomach will make you feel better." His cocky smile and snake eyes sent a chill down my spine.

"Did you party last night? You look pale." He shoved a fork-full of eggs, bit his toast, and downed them with coffee.

"No, no party last night for me." I tried to keep a steady hand as I served the eggs but some fell on the white linen. I picked them up with my fingers and tried to clean up the greasy spot with the napkin, spreading the yellowish spot.

He buttered a piece of toast, and kept eating.

"How is the Porsche running? I just got new tires installed."

Half-chewed toast tumbled inside his mouth.

"Love it." I spoke with my mouth full also.

"You know Miguel and Jose have been with me longer than you. So, count the money better next time, okay?" He pointed between my eyes with his fork.

After the risk of flying around with the accounting book, and all the preparation for my defense, I was dismissed.

"Take the Volvo and tell Jose to take it to the shop. He'll drive you to the airport. Be careful." He left the car keys on the table, got up and went to his room.

I swapped keys and walked out on unsteady legs. The eggs and coffee ran up and down my throat, tempting me to throw up all over the smooth leather seats of his new ride.

I returned to California with the tail between my legs, humiliated and 37,000 reasons to be bitter.

***

Chasing my dream again, in between jobs, I took helicopter flying classes.

The flight school occupied a couple of hangars at the Long Beach Airport. The instructor gave me some ground instruction and we got ready to fly.

It was the same type of helicopter I had taken rides at the plantation. We took off and he flew towards the coast. The sunny afternoon presented a gorgeous scenario as we headed south bordering the coast. On the way back, as we approached some empty fields, the instructor asked me about a procedure called "Autorotation".

"Sure, I have read about it." I didn't remember what it was and didn't want to look stupid.

"Ok, here we go, then…" He cut power and started to descend.

To me it looked like a normal descend to land so it wasn't a big deal.

"And that is what you do when you loose the engine…" He said with a grin as we got to about 50 feet of the ground.

I nodded and looked forward.

He climbed and headed back to the airport.

"Why do you want to learn to fly helicopters?" He chatted.

"Just for fun." I said casually.

"What applications they have for helicopters in Colombia?"

"Crop dusting…my family owns banana plantations…" I started to get annoyed.

"Really?" He looked at me unconvinced.

"Really."

I never came back. He's curiosity spooked me, and I didn't want the extra attention. Fear stealing my dream again.

I didn't want to bring problems, nor give Gil reasons to fire me, but time brought the answers about him and the organization.

A few months later, Gil and I collected $150,000 from a client in San Francisco. It was the first time I've seen him getting involved. We met at a parking structure by the Fisherman's Wharf. He spoke to the client as I stood behind, then he grabbed the duffel bag and threw it casually to me. His cocky attitude and bluntness made me nervous.

We got to the luxurious apartment I've rented overlooking the bay, and while counting the money, I had to go to the bathroom. Usually, nobody leaves the room while counting money, but I trusted him. The final count was $5000 short.

"Let's report it. Let's call the client…" I told him.

"No, you lose it." His snake eyes didn't smile.

"What?" My mind reeled.

"You loose it." He held my gaze.

A chill shot down my spine, and a hot flash hit my brain. *Like that huh…*

A couple of days later, while paying for one of his trademark suede jackets, he pulled a wad of fifties. I had not given him fifties out of the stash. He caught me looking and smiled.

Why would he rip me off? It made no sense, and it wasn't right, but I wanted to continue working. If it cost me five grand, so what, it'll come around.

Just the same, money transformed me. I made ten, twenty thousand dollars a day, worked a couple of weeks, finished the load, and waited, sometimes months, for the next project.

In between jobs, I rented more houses, got communications, and made transportation arrangements. I kept at least three houses at a time, moving around California cities like Garden Grove, Irvine, Fullerton, Huntington Beach, Newport Beach, Laguna Hills, Rowland Heights, Laguna Niguel, Aliso Viejo, Mission Viejo, San Marcos, and San Francisco.

All I had to do was to keep my nose clean when making the deliveries.

We serviced clients in San Diego, Los Angeles and San Francisco. I got calls from clients in San Francisco in the morning, caught a plane, took care of the details of the order over lunch, and flew back. Next day I'd drive up with 20 or 30 kilos. We provided pure product and fast service. A couple of days later I'd drive back to Southern California with the cash.

Then go to San Diego and meet the clients there. The San Diego runs were a little trickier because of the Immigration check point in San Onofre on the drive back, sometimes with money, or even with returned merchandize.

I kept busy under the reins of Gil until we had a disagreement. He had come to California to wait for the load, and one night, I told him that I was going on a date.

"We are waiting for the call to pick up the load anytime, you can't go out," he snapped.

"I am not going to bring her here," I said.

"You can't go out, we are waiting."

"You can't be serious..." Heat rose to my head. *He brings women to the houses...even when we are loaded....*

As if reading my mind, he said. "I am the boss, and you are *not* going out."

I grabbed the car's keys, and walked towards the door. "I will be back in the morning."

"If you go...you are fired."

I looked at him, and walked out. "See you tomorrow." *He's*

got to be kidding. I got in my car, and went out for a night of romance and good food.

The next day, I came to the house, and he opened the front door. "Give me the pager."

"Come on Gil...after all I've done for you." I took a step backwards.

His eyes were wild. "Give me the pager, the call is coming any time, I told you." He moved to block the door.

"Yes, but-"

"Give me the pager."

"No, the pager is in my name." I put my hand over it. "And the houses are on my name also." I stepped forward.

His lips pinched together in a frown, he turned around and went into the house. He returned swiftly and raised his right hand holding my semi-automatic pistol.

I knew it had a bullet in the chamber.

His breathing was heavy.

He pointed it between my eyes, about a foot away, and pulled the trigger. Click.

Time stopped.

I shook my head. "What are you doing? Are you crazy man?" I gave him the beeper and walked out.

I drove back to the house in Garden Grove, sat on the couch and put my head between my hands. *Is he going to send someone to kill me like he did with the rogue worker in Medellín? What is he thinking? He must be going nuts without smoking.*

When I was Gil's bodyguard in Medellín, he had a disagreement with a worker, and in return the disgruntled employee had broken into the warehouse and stole some weapons, and God knows what else.

We were in high alert for a while, and never saw the co-worker again.

Now, I was the disgruntled one, and without his coke to smoke, he was unpredictable and volatile.

I was fired. Better than fired upon, though. *Loyalty didn't pay.*

About three months later, I saw Gil and Jose eating at South Coast Plaza. The Florida crew had conquered California at last. We exchanged greetings, and life went on. No hard feelings. The key now was to keep working without touching his clients. That'd get me killed for sure.

About a week later, as I walked by a shopping center, I saw Sam. He seemed to be making a delivery, and had a passenger with him, provably his new trainee, and most likely, his replacement. He never contacted me.

I bought a new Chevy Blazer, and moved into a condo in Laguna Niguel, about ten minutes from Salt Creek, my favorite beach near the Dana Point harbor. The change of pace was refreshing and brought sunshine into my life.

I met Tammy at that beach, a gorgeous blue-eyed girl, with a fit body and a sharp mind. She and her roommates were lying by the lifeguard tower, right down the access ramp. It was my favorite spot also, and I had seen them there before. We'd exchanged a few words, "What time is it?" or "Could you watch my things for a while?", but nothing more.

That summer day, as I picked up my things and started up the long ramp towards the parking lot, she walked just ahead, and I offered to help her with the beach chair. We talked, and walked. What a smile. My heart pumped faster and felt out of breath. As we got to her car, I asked if she wanted to go to the movies, and we got a date.

We went to the theaters at the Mission Viejo Mall, and after the movie, as I was opening the door of the truck for her, we kissed for the first time. Those full sexy lips were soft and sweet. Her trimmed body, felt just right in my arms, and her short curly hair, silky, as I softly pulled it. We went to her house and she introduced me to her roommates. They seemed to approve of me.

I will never forget those big blue eyes, blue like the sky. I will never forget that first kiss. It was beautiful. She was beautiful.

Her easy going demeanor made me feel real. But, I wasn't real. I was full of lies. I was an emerald merchant without stones, a jewelry designer without a studio, I was a fake. Yes, I had worked with emeralds, and yes I was a jewelry designer, but the reality was very different now. Who was I really?

If I had been capable of loving someone then, I'd say, I loved her.

I wanted to forget my situation, but reality knocked on my door. Money was running out. I did a couple of small jobs but it was hard to get solid connections without going back to Medellín. Uncertain of the future, I packed my things and shipped them. My first chapter in the U.S. had come to an end.

Saying good-bye to Tammy was heartbreaking. I remember those tears the night before I went back to Colombia. Big eyes shed big tears. We dined at a restaurant on the hill overlooking the Dana Point marina, a romantic evening under a cloud of doom.

I wanted to feel sad, but there seemed to be a connection missing in my brain, instead I felt her sadness. *Is there something wrong with me? Here is this gorgeous woman crying because I am leaving, and...I feel a hole in my chest...it's better for her that I go away.*

In Medellín, I settled in the restaurant again. I tried to adapt, but the California life had gotten under my skin. So, after almost a year, I started making plans to go back.

I made new connections, and partied. In those times of uncontrollable debauchery I built a reputation between the mafia circles. They named me *El Loco*, the Mad Man, and they avoided me.

The truth of the matter was that I felt out of place everywhere, so I drowned the feeling on tequila tides, and sought love in revolving arms.

Almost out of money, and tired of the pistolero atmosphere - carrying a gun and pretending I was a tough guy - it got old for me. I sold my diamond ring, and with ten thousand dollars in my pocket, I headed back to the U.S. to start my own operation.

Back in California, I rented an apartment in Fullerton, got a Volkswagen Jetta, and reported to Colombia that I was ready to roll.

7 THE CONTRACTOR

Finally one of the connections came through, and I started picking up money. Once or twice a week I picked up cash, and the rest of the week I partied.

One night at the Red Onion, a Mexican Grill in Costa Mesa, I was dancing with the owner of a modeling agency I had met while looking for a side job. As we swirled, I looked towards the booths along the wall, and there was Tammy with her friends.

I went by her table to find a hostile environment.

"What are you doing here? I thought you were in Colombia." Tammy said.

"I got here a couple of days ago."

She stared at her drink.

"You called me once in *a year*. I thought you weren't coming back."

"I wasn't, but...I can explain." The truth of the matter was that I didn't even know why I hadn't called her.

"Nothing to explain, you seemed to be having fun there." She made circles with her margarita glass.

"Leather pants, silk shirt, pony tail...you look like a gigolo." Her friend pointed an accusing finger.

"I *had* a pony tail before-" I snapped.

"She is kind of old for you..." The other friend hissed.

"Let's go." Tammy finished her drink and got up.

They followed.

I trailed behind them to the parking lot.

The friends ran interference in front of me.

I walked around them. "Can I call you?" I walked by her side, and reached for her elbow.

"No. That is not a good idea." She pulled away.

"Please. Tammy, I'm sorry I didn't call...Please, Tammy I missed you."

She got her keys out and opened the door of her car, "No. It's better this way," held my gaze, and got in.

"Please Tammy. Give me a chance to make it up to you...please."

They got in her car. Those huge blue eyes looked back through the closed window. She pulled out of the parking spot and drove away.

"Hey. Tammy...Tammy." I waved and ran behind. Then, I watched the car drive into the night.

The next morning I called her number but was disconnected, then drove to their house in Dana Point but they didn't live there anymore.

I regretted not valuing her. It was the best for her after all. I didn't deserve her.

Life went on. I had to come up again. What did I have to offer her anyway?

I continued the cash pick ups, but I knew this branch had more risk. People delivering reported more than delivered. I suspected the false reports were tests, other times, they were just *avionadas,* pulling fast ones.

During this time the cartel separated the cash operations from the product distribution. Too many people were going down with the drugs and the money. These transitions presented new opportunities for infiltrations though. Bankers and business owners jumped at the sight of quick profits but were didn't weigh the dangers involved. I didn't trust them. I knew they'd turn at the drop of a dime.

There was more money and less exposure moving drugs, so I continued seeking connections for distribution. After a while, I got 20 kilos but I couldn't find buyers because the acid level was too high, which made it gooey. I tried drying it but it didn't work. The owner started to get restless and pressured me to pay for it, or to pass it to someone else that had the market for that kind of merchandise. He told me that with the crack epidemic, that kind of cocaine was in high demand in certain circles. The ratio of return when turned to crack was very high. So, all I got from that operation was a hole in nose, that stuff burned.

I decided to take a vacation, so I flew to Miami to deliver $50,000 and went to visit a high school friend. I spent a couple days with Santos, flew ultralights, and partied. I borrowed one of his cars and drove up to Fort Lauderdale where I settled at the Hilton, rested, and got ready to party. The concierge pointed me to the best disco in town, and there I went. The place had several dance floors, VIP rooms, and was filled with tourists and college crowds going crazy. It was Spring Break. I got a drink and started to scan the scenery…She was standing against the wall.

The right size, the right attitude, a little arrogant, lots of blond curly hair, and a small pretty mouth. I was a sucker for curly hair.

"Hey, wanna dance?"

She looked me up and down, gave me a little crooked smile, half smiling, half pouting, and batted those eyelashes like a bat in a hurricane. "Why not…" She put her empty glass on a nearby table and led to the dance floor.

"Hum, you *can* dance…" she teased.

Vanessa was a gymnast, and knew how to dance. Flirty and hot, sexy and classy, I was hooked.

Chemistry floating in the air, we took a brake.

I ordered the first bottle of Dom Perignon, and we were directed to the VIP room with its private dance floor. Not so crowded, and smoothed out by bottles of the bubbly Dom, we danced the night away.

She didn't let me go away.

We had a couple of wild nights and good days, and then I went back to Miami to help Santos with some business.

Afterwards, Santos invited me to test an airboat he had

built with an ultralight engine. Usually airboats have an airplane engine much larger than the one we were testing. We went to his shop, loaded it in a trailer, and took off. We got to the everglades and lowered the prototype on the water. He drove it for a while and then it was my turn.

He told me. "Don't floor the throttle for a long time. It's a two stroke engine, let it breathe, otherwise you'll burn it."

I did as I was told, and had a great time as the flat bottom hull skipped over water. The driver's seat was on front of the propeller casing, so the engine's roar and the wind going through, made it a unique experience. It was a real rush.

Then, it was Santo's turn again. This time he didn't do as he had told me. He pushed the accelerator lever to the end, engine roaring, full throttle, pedal to the metal, on, and on, and on, until puff. The engine burned out.

I turned around and looked at him. "What happened with 'let the engine breathe'?"

He chuckled.

That was the kind of guy he was, always smiling, always a good attitude. Santos was a good friend. Racing, flying, or fixing machines, I wanted to be like him. But, now, our future looked grim.

It was about five in the evening, alligators' dinner time.

A couple of nights before, I had watched with Vanessa a National Geographic documentary about the everglades' alligator and crocodile population. The creatures splashed around as they held their victims within those massive jaws. Those monsters made sounds between a bark and the mooing sound of a cow, a very scary growl. Now, the images played in my photographic mind with vivid effect.

I looked around, but everything seemed the same -dark brown water and tall bush forever. We pulled the boat by grabbing the tall vegetation around us. The sharp edges cut my hands and I hoped the smell of blood didn't reach a hungry gator.

I waved my muddy and bloody shirt to an airplane flying by, but it continued its slow and lazy cruise purring softly. I looked at it glide away against the blasting sun. Santos looked at me with a half-smile, and continued pulling the boat forward, little by little.

Then, he gave up also.

Night fell around the unlimited pond filled with hungry creatures known and unknown. The half-moon illuminated the rippling water and the vegetation's sounds played with my mind.

Santos had a *brilliant* idea. "We can jump in the water and pull the boat to the shore."

"Really, which way?" I looked around.

"There." He pointed.

"Go ahead." I muttered.

Santos got in the water, as I climbed onto the mesh that covered the propeller. "I'll watch for the alligators." I scanned the dark pond.

He jumped back in the boat and chuckled. "Let's take the propeller out, and the chair off, so we can row with them."

I climbed down from my safety perch, and got busy with the chair as he unbolted the propeller.

We rowed with them until we saw the shoreline.

"We can walk from here." He got in the water.

I got in after him, and as he stabbed the bottom with the propeller, I followed pulling the boat.

The water was warm and dark, I could see the shore and we moved swiftly. My heart pumped as my mind ran through the images of dark beasts swimming under, which, thanks to National Geographic, were as clear as if I were seated in front of the TV. The scenes of screaming bodies being broken in the mouths of gators, or Bambi's mother looking from the shore as Bambi stuck its tongue out and flapped around in the monster's mouth.

The shore was now about twenty yards away and I wondered how fast a gator could do those twenty yards. I figured, faster than I could. Much faster. If only I could run on water.

I felt like a coward, no bravado, no tough guy, just trying to survive the night. It is amazing how human nature changes when facing death. Out there we were nobody, and nobody knew we were there.

When we finally reached the shore, we lay on the grass watching the stars. Then we pulled the boat out of the water, and walked towards the road. I didn't care if I had to walk all the way to Miami.

After a while, we found a road and followed it towards the place we had left the cars. I had no idea where we were, and I don't know how Santos could find the way at night.

One Good Samaritan in an old Toyota pick-up truck stopped. My white polo shorts and shirt were torn, and covered with mud and blood. The driver didn't seem to notice the condition of these pilgrims, or the propeller I was carrying as a souvenir. He told us to jump in the back, and there we went.

He dropped us by our cars and we drove into the night, Santos to his home in Coconut Grove, and me, back to my honey-bunny in Fort Lauderdale.

I got to her condo and knocked on the door, holding a bottle of Dom and a dozen red roses.

Vanessa opened the door. "There you are-" She looked me up and down, and smiled. "Need a nurse?"

I handed her the roses, and stumbled after her.

She didn't ask any questions, just kept smiling that crocked smile of hers, and lead me to the bathroom to give me a much-needed bath while cleaning and bandaging my bloody hands. She brought me back to life.

After a couple of days recuperating, I invited her to come to California, but she refused. So I headed back to Coconut Grove, gave Santos his car back, and went to the airport.

As I walked around before my flight, someone called to me. I turned to find Vanessa trailing a small suitcase.

Shaking her curls, she pouted and said; "Well, are you gonna get my ticket or what?"

I smiled, reached for her, and gave her a long kiss. "Let's do that." I grabbed her hand and pulled her toward the ticket counter.

We got to California, picked up my car at extended parking, and drove to the small apartment in Garden Grove where I was living under an alias. As we got to the carport I noticed my motorcycle gone, only a piece of the ignition switch on the floor. I had made a mistake though. The bike was under my real name so I could not report it to the police. Well, you win some and lose some.

A week later, we moved to San Mateo where I had some connections. I was trying to get hired to handle their distribution. It didn't work. Instead, they fronted me a kilo. I broke it into ounces, and took it to Santa Cruz where I had a friend.

Vanessa knew about the money transportation to Miami, but, she had no idea what I was doing in Santa Cruz, or so I thought.

We went to Lake Tahoe, rented a condo by the lake, and in the spur-of-the-moment decided to get married. I went into a jewelry store in a casino and bought the rings, then we drove to a chapel and tied the knot. We did some skiing and relaxed for a week, then headed back down. The honeymoon was over. We bought a cat, and named him *Diablo*.

I was doing jewelry design on the side, and used the cocaine profits to buy equipment to set a studio in the second bedroom of our apartment. I enrolled at the local college for jewelry classes, and A & P - Airframe and Powerplant - an aircraft mechanic class, another of my dreams. I went to the first few classes but there were a couple of guys that looked like federal agents, so I never came back. Fear took my most precious goals.

The relationship deteriorated because of my drinking and the trips to Santa Cruz, money problems delivered the final blow. I spent money quicker than I made it. The marriage went south and my ex-wife east with *Diablo.*

I continued my business in Santa Cruz and partied hard with my friends there.

After a tequila-drenched mourning for my failed marriage, and a few one-night stands, I met TC, a long-legged-surfer-girl with silky blond hair and blue eyes, a real looker. She was a waitress at the pier in Santa Cruz and a good friend of Rocky, a Colombian I hanged out with there. I wanted her so bad, that I made one of the biggest mistakes in the business. I involved her, offered her a job. She in return volunteered information about some heavy weapons in the market. I bought a MAC-10 with silencer from her. I called my new toy "La Muda", The Mute, because of the silencer, and it became my favorite companion.

At the same time, Simon, a friend from the plantation area, was planning to open a distribution center in Southern California. He was connected with BIG people in Medellín, and we joined forces. He had the backing, and I had the experience in the U.S.

We were close friends, but the similar taste in women brought a veiled rivalry between Simon and me. Often we found ourselves with the same girlfriend. Women played the male's primitive desire to conquer, and then shifted the page of the menu, dropping one of us with cold indifference. And, we thought we were the conquerors.

Simon' father, owner of several businesses in town, inspired me fear and respect. He was a man of few words. His gaze gave me a desire to run away and change my ways, feeling that quickly dimmed by the appearance of his daughters.

Simon had five attractive sisters that managed the family businesses under the tyrannical gaze of the Don. I frequented their *Gallera*, the cockfight ring, where I learned to dance salsa. Coached by La Negra, my favorite of the daughters, we swirled in the dance floor and sweated entangled in passionate arms carried by the provocative tunes. The disapproval of the Don and Simon, gave my relationship with La Negra a delicious mystery. Nevertheless, Simon and I had a strong bond.

La Negra had called me to Simon' rescue one night, as I danced at one of the discos that bordered the town's plaza.

She ran in, and sat on the booth on front of me. "Mono, they are going to kill him…" She gave a cold smile to my companion. More like a silent growl.

Did I hear a hiss?

"It's Simon, they are going to kill him…they have machetes…"

"What is it? Who?" I looked into her wild black eyes.

"The Trilla brothers…" She tugged on my hand.

I grabbed her hand and got up, pulling her. "Let's go."

We ran out of the disco.

"Over there." She pointed to the end of the block.

We ran.

I opened by handbag and pulled my father's .38 Smith & Wesson revolver. As we turned around the corner I saw Simon with his sidekick Riggo. They were surrounded by five thugs. I knew this feud went way back and I didn't want to get involved, but my bond with La Negra called for action. She was more than a good friend.

The thugs yelled obscenities and swung their machetes. Simon waved a small knife, back to back with Riggo, ready to jump into action, a deadly dance soon to unravel.

I could see a few bystanders back in the dark alley.

One of the thugs saw me approach, and turned my way.

"Bang!" I shot into the air, and pointed to the attackers, coming to a halt by Simon' side.

I cursed them. "Get out of here or I'll kill you!"

In the small town, we all knew of each other. I have seen Simon archrival, a skinny short ragged youngster, now holding a large machete. Simon had stabbed him in a quarrel a few months back, and now he wanted revenge.

"The police." One of the bystanders yelled, and disappeared into the dark.

"The police, the police...let's get out of here." La Negra shouted from the corner.

The thugs ran down the alley and into an empty lot across the street.

I threw the revolver into the nearby bushes and ran back into the town's plaza. I looked back and saw Simon and Riggo speeding away from the plaza.

"No, let's go this way..." I yelled.

"But...but the police..." Riggo stammered.

I waved them to follow. "Let's move."

We walked around the corner.

The policemen came running.

"What's going on?" One said as they halted a few yards away.

"Who is shooting?" An older officer shouted.

"I don't know...it came from over there officer." I pointed

towards the empty lot. "We were going home but decided to go back this way. I don't know…"

He looked at the tall bushes of the empty lot.

"Let me see your handbag." A young officer reached out toward me.

"Here you go…" I opened it for him to look inside.

He gave me a cautious gaze. "Give it to me." He expended his hand.

"Here…"

He looked inside, and took my wallet out, checked my driver's license, put it all back inside, and handed me the handbag. "Thanks Mr. Rauu."

The locals had a hard time pronouncing my name.

"Get out of here." The older policeman said.

"Yes, Sir." Simon walked away with Riggo behind.

The policemen went into the alley, and we walked into the night.

I waited for a while and went back looking for the revolver. In the heat of the moment I've forgotten where I threw it. I searched the bushes, and one of the bystanders appeared again and helped me. These kids seemed to follow us around. Another one stomped on the knee high vines.

"Here it is!" He gave a shout of victory waving the big revolver.

"Thanks." I put the gun inside my handbag.

I walked back to my pick-up parked on front of the disco, and drove to the plantation.

After the sale of the plantation we stayed in touch, and now, we were up to real mischief.

When I contacted Simon, he told me to get a couple of houses in Southern California for a big operation with the big boss. The opportunity I waited for so long finally knocked on my door.

8 THE BIG LEAGUES

Colombia was going through one of the bloodiest times in its history. The boss of bosses, Pablo Escobar was making deals with the government, turning close associates in, and assassinating government officials. Simon's big project connected us to Pablo through one of his lieutenants.

Regardless of these background factors the project steadily took form. I moved from northern California, and TC came lured by my promise of the car of her dreams. We moved into a three bedroom house in Mission Viejo, about 50 miles south of Los Angeles.

I got a new cat, named him *Diablo*, again, and got him *Angel*, his companion. My furry black-smoke Persians left hair everywhere, but I loved them so much, I didn't care.

After we got settled, I reported to Simon and he came from Medellín. My first big job, eight hundred kilos for Pablo Escobar, the big boss of the Medellín Cartel, *El Doctor,* the most dangerous and prominent crime figure of the time.

Now I was in the shadow of a monster. Pablo's assassinations of judges, several high ranking police officers, a

Minister of Justice, and candidate for the presidency, labeled him "Public Enemy Number One in the world". The bombings in Colombia killed lots of innocent people including the passengers of an airliner.

Enforcement because someone talked, was one thing - one thing I hoped I never had to do - but killing innocent people was senseless and bad for business.

TC got her black Mustang convertible. I got a Caprice to cruise around, and two Chevrolet Suburbans fitted to carry up to a thousand kilos. I tried to keep a personal car and house, so I didn't use my Audi for business. Diverting from my regulations and security measures, made me nervous, having TC and Simon knowing all my whereabouts broke my circle of protection.

Simon put together another crew to handle the money, Louie and Gio. I did not trust Louie, an attorney. My theory was that attorneys were only needed when someone goes to jail, and the prospect of having one in the crew made me uneasy. I told Simon that I didn't want to have anything to do with these two characters. I could feel the heat.

I got another house up in Rowland Heights to store the merchandise, while I lived with TC in Mission Viejo. It turned out to be a bad decision because I didn't know that area that well, or how hot it was. My comfort zone was South Orange County. I knew it like the palm of my hand.

After waiting a few months, the call finally came. Simon and I met with the people who brought the load across the border, and agreed to meet the next day for the delivery. They insisted that I come alone with a rental truck. I didn't want to expose the Suburbans to an unknown crew, and not knowing how the merchandize was packed, all I could get on such a short notice was a bright yellow rental truck.

The transporters wanted their money up front, so Simon made the necessary phone calls to the office in Medellín, we went to Los Angeles to pick up one million in cash, and delivered it to them.

This deal didn't fit my modus operandi. I didn't like the changes but it was out of my control, besides, the one with the load sets the rules.

Some people accepted suggestions about the delivery, but I had to be careful because if something went wrong, I would be the first suspect and the first to get tortured to death.

I met with the transporters at a restaurant in Diamond Bar, about 10 miles from the stash house. One of the guys was to go with me, and *he* wanted to drive. I brought a semi-automatic pistol with me, even though I knew that if something went wrong, there would be very little time to do anything.

So I rode with the guy. He was from another country, not a Colombian, and I didn't feel comfortable with him at all. He drove and sang in a Middle Eastern language, like a snake enchanter. He was making me nervous and the idea of shooting him crossed my mind.

He got off the freeway, drove to an area of small ranches, and turned into a dirt driveway. I could see the small run-down house in the middle of an empty field, and an old RV on the driveway.

We got out of the truck as his boss came out of the house, exchanged greetings, and then got right to business. I climbed inside the back of the truck and the chanting driver, quiet now, passed the big canvas bags and I pushed them forward towards the front of the truck's box. I felt like a sitting duck. The only insurance I had of not being killed by them was that they were not clear of the obligation to the shippers until Simon confirmed the delivery.

The chanting driver finished and walked away without a final song. I jumped out of the truck, closed the back door and latched it, shook hands with the boss, and drove out. Now I was a moving duck.

I checked the mirrors for a tail and I found my way into the net of Southern California freeways. The yellow truck made me feel foolish, since I was used to blend with my fleet of vehicles specially picked out. My professionalism and training out of the window, but there I went.

I got to the house in Azusa and backed up the truck against the garage door. Simon helped me to unload and get the canvas bags inside. I didn't like the neighbors seeing the truck and no furniture coming out. Little details like that are the ones that get you busted.

We counted the load, but I didn't feel comfortable leaving it at that location. A few days before, I'd noticed a cheap woman's shoe under the couch and I suspected that Simon had a party there.

At least Simon listened to my advice. It was his first operation in this area. His territory was handling business in Medellín and he did not speak English. I was surprised that he'd hung around this long. I guessed that this was a new connection for him also.

I didn't care who his connection was, I'd met one of the bosses at busy office in downtown Medellín on a previous trip. The lieutenant interviewed me and told me to get ready. The next weekend after the meeting, Simon had invited me to a ranch in

Santa Fe de Antioquia, a little town nearby Medellín, where he introduced me to more of his *friends*. I never knew which one was higher in the chain of command, nor did I ask if he was working with different groups.

After recounting the kilos and classifying them by the different markings –some had a caterpillar, others a penny- stamped on the wrapping, we loaded the suburban and took the load to the Mission Viejo house. Only TC knew this home. I liked working alone, no workers, no loose ends, no one to kill for having sticky hands, and most of all, no one to put a bullet in the back of my head to keep it all. Me, my woman, and my partner, already too many, but it had to do.

Safety procedures crowded my every day life. I didn't trust cellular phones to make appointments for pick-ups and deliveries, much less to call Colombia. So, I gave a weekly list of ten payphones to the office in Colombia with an assigned code. I would page the code from an assigned cellular and they would call that payphone within 15 minutes, that way, I would only have to wait at the appointed phone only five minutes. If the page was intercepted, it would have a list of worthless numbers.

I figured that it would be easy for law enforcement agencies to keep track of payphones that people frequented to call Colombia. I also thought that some numbers were particularly hot in their list. All it would take to pick up a tail was to page a hot number and wait at that same payphone for the police to come.

Paranoia is a monkey hard to shake. Like a tick ripped of its host leaving its head inside the body spreading darkness into the soul, paranoia stays after the storm, a personal cloud covering the sun.

Even driving down the freeway and watching the camera

on the overpasses gave me the feeling of being watched. I lived on stage 24/7. My whole life became an act for the eye in the sky.

The following days, I looked at the stacked boxes by the dining room wall. Moving boxes, filled with demons imported from the jungles of South America. Like the Blood Diamonds, these were Blood Bricks from Colombia. Shiny scales, Satan's tears to bring misery to all who touch them and used them, affecting previous and following generations.

We started delivering after a cooling period of a couple of days. In the morning we planned the lunch deliveries, and during the evening we made appointments for the next day.

The money-crew started to make up stories and darkness crept in my heart. How wicked can one become. Like a drop of ink in a glass of water, my heart in darkness dwelling, in hardness growing. I suspected they wanted to rip us off.

They told Simon that one of their apartments had been searched by the police, and that the Caprice under TC's name was in the parking garage. There was one hundred and thirty grand in the trunk. Their story had too many holes, and my German logic sparked doubt. If the police had raided the apartment, they would have checked the car on the assigned spot, it didn't make sense. I was not afraid, I was enraged. That was an insult to my intelligence.

We sat a meeting that night at an Argentinean Restaurant in Riverside, about an hour from my center of operations. I told Simon to invite Gio into the suburban to talk, while I sat in the back seat. I intended to get the truth out of him.

Pablo certainly could take the hit, but his tainted tentacles had entered and contaminated my mind with his signature of violence that sat him apart from the rest.

Gio didn't get into the SUV. He stood safely away from the Suburban stealing glances at the tinted windows. Simon signaled me and we went into the restaurant and planned a rescue operation. I proposed to Simon that TC and I would rescue the money for half of the loot. We negotiated and finally agreed on fee. Gio and Louie looked disappointed. TC and I went back to Orange County to do the job. I was glad to have extra sets of spare keys for all the cars.

The apartment was on Beach Boulevard, a busy street, in Huntington Beach, so we'd agreed to do it at night. I drove the Mustang by the apartments, stopped, and pretended to be arguing by the side of the road. She got out of the car yelling and waved me off. I drove away.

She was a tough woman, fearless and crazy, or at least crazy, that much I know. I took off and saw her in the rear view mirror as she climbed a rocky pillar that held the metal fence surrounding the apartment's parking lot. She jumped in and disappeared in the darkness. If she was stopped, at least the car was on her name.

I went into a convenience store down the road to wait. Eating Twinkies with milk until I felt nauseous, I looked down the street for the loaded Caprice to appear. She was taking too long. I liked her, it was one of those love/hate relationships. We loved each other late at night, and fought the rest of the time.

The clerk was starting to look at me with suspicion, when, at last, the big sedan came into the parking lot. She got out, gave me the keys and drove off in her Mustang. We met at home and split the bounty.

Simon was happy and so were we. Gio and Louie didn't count on the crazy California girl that rescued their keep. I never knew anything else about the "raided" apartment, and kept my distance from them. The operation went on, and we continued making deliveries. I told TC to give the Caprice to her sister, and got new phones and pagers, just in case. We had three of the foot long Motorolas –cellulars had just came out- and we kept them as sanitized as possible by never calling the office in Colombia with the phones we used to communicate during the operation. I assumed the people down south weren't cautious on their phone conversations, as it had happened before while speaking in person. Some even bragged in public places.

Like the time I was with Simon in Colombia and we met with the *Hut*, one of his connections, at a small but elegant restaurant in El Poblado. I sat on a side table as the Hut's bodyguards sat at another table behind him. He started yelling about twenty five kilos lost in New York and that Simon was responsible for the full payment.

At lunch time, the place was full of young executives and couples having a gourmet meal, and as *the Hut* raised his voice, they gave us scared side glances. I wanted to hide under the table. I could not believe this guy, talking about business like that. I guessed it was one of the things that started to get Colombians tired, the boldness and the violence. Many people are involved directly or indirectly, but nobody wants it screamed about in the middle of a peaceful lunch.

Now, with the issue with the money crew, my nerves were raw.

Simon and I spent the free time carefully planning the deliveries. We'd tell the client to come to a specific area and call my pager from a payphone, never to call from cellulars. We knew the prefixes of the payphones of those predetermined areas, and timed the clients' drive to the final meeting place. If the person took too long to drive to the appointed restaurant, we'd cancel the meeting.

Simon dropped me off to meet the clients and get their cars to load them. He, then, would drive with the client making sure he did not make any phone calls. I'd take their car, load it, and drop it at an agreed location where Simon would later pick me up. We could deliver two or three-hundred kilos a day.

Let the money roll. Good times don't last though.

The last delivery of the load, I was supposed to meet the client at a restaurant in south Mission Viejo. I came in the restaurant, ordered and sat, then noticed some patrons not enjoying the meal but looking at the crowd. I was determined to make the delivery anyway. I made contact, got in the client's car and drove around to make sure there were no problems. All seemed to be going fine until I got near the house and opened the garage door. The police helicopter zoomed over the roof.

I drove in the garage and figured that if the car had a tracking device I had to get out quickly. I loaded, drove out, and took it to the drop area. This was too close for comfort. I knew that they had me identified or at least the location of the stash house, but somehow I had been able to make the delivery.

It was time to take a vacation, time to run.

JACK E. RAUSCH

9 THE BIG TAIL

Simon didn't like the idea. I told him he was welcome to stay. I packed the Suburban and he reluctantly agreed to go with us to Big Bear. It was ski season.

We skied our way up the Californian mountain range. Two weeks at Big Bear, the closest ski resort to Los Angeles area, another two weeks at Mammoth Mountain, and then we finished our skiing tour at Lake Tahoe a gorgeous resort town at the border with Nevada. Nice snow, beautiful sunshine, and a hot tail.

One day, coming down the slope I skidded to a stop to take a rest. Taking in the beautiful scenery of the snow covered mountain peppered by pine trees down to the lake, feeling the cold breeze and looking at gorgeous people having a good time, I heard someone skid to a stop next to me. I turned to find a tall, clean cut blond man. He smiled and said; "It's hot in the fast lane, isn't it?" Smiling again, he took off down the mountain, leaving me frozen in place as a chill ran down my spine.

Not good, if the law was that close, I was finished. I watched the clean-cut-tall-blond-guy slide down the mountain, like a farmer watches the flooding river take his crops with the raging waters, my Doom's Day.

They were close and not happy. *Was there a rat?* By now, another guy and his girlfriend had joined the entourage. I was hardened, but not stupid. How long was the heat going to stick around? I was finished. *What was I going to do now? Had the office in Colombia sold us out?* It had happened to bigger fishes, given up by their partners in exchange for immunity. Carlos Lehder, one of the transportation guys, claimed that Pablo Escobar had given him up. *Did they give us up to get a bigger load to go through? Could it be possible?* I felt trapped. Restless. I wanted my guns, but I didn't want to drive around with them, and after all, we were on *vacation. They are waiting for us to get loaded again...*

Greed had blinded me. I could have retired and gone to college. I had started classes to become an airplane technician, and helicopter flight training, but something always spooked my away from the good path. I had the tools for jewelry design, but the lure of the money, and the thrill of the operations kept bringing me back to this evil brew. Now, I had come to a blind spot in my life with a hole in my pockets. The money went out faster than it came in, disappeared in a rush. Too much Dom Perignon and alligator shoes, the money walked.

After the close encounter, the group split. Simon went to Medellín, and the other guy and his girlfriend disappeared into the woodwork where they'd come from.

TC and I drove back to Mission Viejo. Sore and stressed regardless of the vacation, TC and I were having problems. My cocaine use had been escalating, making me a persona non grata. Paranoia wasn't a sweet companion. I interrogated her after long hours of partying, questioning her comings and goings, and double questioning everything she'd said. But that was not the problem, questioning was the second stage in my delusions. The first stage was to bring the guns out. I'd put on my military field jacket, fill the pockets with bullet clips, stick a semi-automatic pistol in my waistband, and keep the MAC-10 machine-gun with the silencer attached resting quietly on my lap. The charming Latino turned into a heavily-armed, sweaty, psycho.

I'd seat with TC talking about an incident that I would dissect, analyze, and question every part. Phones were dissected, and every piece smashed with a hammer to make sure it would not transmit secret information again.

My suspicions that she wanted some rope, some freedom, some taste of a normal life again, brought about horrible fights. I kept her too tight, yes I understood that she wanted some space, but this was not the time to see her go and spill the operations' details back in her hometown. My inability to trust made things worse.

We got in an argument coming down from the mountains and were determined to end the relationship as soon as we got to Orange County. It was a long drive. Coming down the Interstate 5 we talked, made up, and continued down to Mission Viejo. Carnal problems quickly fixed by the flesh, a bandage on a putrefying corpse.

Back in Orange County things were calm for a while. We went to the beach and to Lake Elsinore to ride the Jet Ski. And then they were there, undercover agents appeared to be everywhere.

One day we went to Los Angeles to visit TC's sister, and while driving through downtown, as we stopped at an intersection, I looked up, and a helicopter was hovering over us, right above the office buildings. I felt uneasy. The heat sent a chill through my bones. We drove to Marina del Rey, and as we sat at the Red Onion Restaurant to have lunch, the same helicopter flew by again.

The next day, I spotted two Chevrolet Camaros, a blue and a brown. I signaled to make a left turn and the blue got on my right side turning lane. The street where he supposed to be turning to was closed. He was in the wrong lane. I looked at him, made eye contact, smiled nodding towards the closed road, and made the turn when the light changed.

Later that afternoon, as I was cruising down Newport Boulevard in Tustin, I saw the brown Camaro behind me. Again I made a U turn and he followed, I got to the intersection and saw the turning light about to turn red and went for it. He did it too. Now it was on. I drove into the parking lot of a convenience store in the corner and got out of the car as the detective pulled in too. I walked up to him and got in his face, "Why are you following me?"

"I don't know what you are talking about, sir."

"I saw you and your partner in the blue Camaro by my house this morning."

"Sorry, I…I don't know what you're talking about…" He went around me and got inside the store.

I had to get out of town for good, there was nowhere to hide. Confirmed, I had a big tail.

I decided to go to Colombia to cool down. Simon had been pressing me to get ready for another load. I called him about the tail and to tell him I was going to Medellín. He didn't like the news. Something was terribly wrong. Another sign I didn't pay attention to.

When I started working in the U.S. in 1984, if someone called the heat, everyone would split. Phones changed, cars and locations abandoned, and after that, the person would go through a period of testing with small jobs, if he was lucky. Most of the time, he'd be out of business, which was actually, the wise thing to do. Quit and run.

TC and I put the furniture and cars in storage, and took off, cats and all, to cloudy and dangerous Medellín, to find a dark horizon in the general scene of the Cartel. These were trying times and I didn't know what would happen, or how long I had to stay there.

One night, TC and I were at a nightclub dancing and having a good time. We sat at the bar on the second floor facing the stairs. I always tried to sit against a wall and facing the doors, close to escape routes, even though I didn't have enemies. Suddenly, I felt a hand on my shoulder and tried to turn but the grip was hard. The Hut, Simon' boss, held me tight. *Where did he come from with all his bodyguards?* I could see, by the corner of my eye, at least three guys behind him, and I figured there were another two behind me. I knew the club was owned by the Cartel, and that this places usually had secret doors and rooms, but this time he caught me by surprise.

"What are you doing here, Mono?" His hot breath blew on my right ear.

I turned, he wasn't smiling. "I told Simon I had a problem..." I tried to move but his heavy bulk leaned on me.

"You're supposed to be there and ready." He sat down on the stool next to mine. His eyes didn't match the smile. He looked like an overweight hyena ready to jump.

"There was no way to get a load out...It would have gone down. You'd had lost your load." "Mono you have to go and receive the next shipment. It should deliver anytime." He got up and stood close to me again.

I pulled a nasal inhaler and sprayed inside my plugged nose. "I had to leave...the police..."

He took the inhaler from me and turning it up-side down squirted into his nose. He coughed. "This –he cursed- is not good." He drank of my glass. "What are you going to do?"

"Don't turn the inhaler down, you have to hold it right side up, and squeeze, so it sprays." I ignored the question.

He cursed again, and shoved the inhaler in my hand. "I got to go." He stormed out, followed by his bodyguards.

This was no good. I hoped my refusal didn't get me killed. Were they trying to set me up? How was Pablo going to take it? TC didn't say a word. She just sat there like a bar's permanent fixture. I ordered another round of drinks to give the Hut time to leave, and then we went home. I had an empty feeling in my stomach. *It was time to get out of town.*

Uneasiness nagged me the rest of the week. Something was wrong and I didn't know what to make of it. *Was Simon working two offices? How come the Hut didn't know about the heat and the too-close-for-comfort-situations?* I thought that the Hut would agree and be grateful.

I didn't want the drama or a bullet on my back. I was on my own. There was no loyalty, and I felt exposed.

To make matters worse, there were all kinds of groups against the Medellín cartel at that time. Pablo's associates were being hunted by Los Pepes, *Perseguidos por Pablo Escobar*, persecuted by Pablo, a group of powerful people that had lost a family member to Pablo's violence, or have been threatened by him. Law enforcement groups offered a million dollars reward for information of his whereabouts, and in retaliation Pablo was paying one million pesos for each policeman killed. People died by the dozens daily.

I heard rumors of Pablo's *invitations* to meetings where the guests were not allowed to leave until each one donated millions of dollars to finance the war with the Cali Cartel and the government.

To top it off, the partying with TC in Medellín also brought some unwanted attention. She was a sensation, her almost white blond hair and the body to go with it created some situations for me. My girlfriends were challenged. One night, at a bar, one of them rubbed my leg with her foot under the table, but when I looked at her, she was flirting with TC.

She was too notorious. Things got bad at a horse show. Because of my German ancestry, I don't look like a Colombian. As we walked to the sitting area, I noticed we'd gotten the attention of a clutter of people. The *Big Guy,* surrounded by women, within a circle of bodyguards, said something to the guys next to him and they looked our way. Two guys got up, came down the stairs, and toward us on the walkway.

As they passed by, one bumped me hard turning me sideways. My sport coat opened revealing my gun in the side-holster.

I nodded and said, "Excuse me brother." My local accent giving them some peace, but I still gave them the attitude of someone connected.

I doubted a gringo in his right mind walked among that crowd.

One of them looked at the group and nodded. A silent permission was given me to watch their horses' parade. Our body parts were not going to end up in trash bags. We lived another day.

Time to leave town. No place to hide.

10 THE BIG BOSS

The next day we went out with Simon and his girlfriend. He invited us to Kevin's a nightclub at the outskirts of Medellín. As we drove in the parking lot, a battalion of bodyguards armed machine guns and hand radios surrounded the huge complex. I tried to play cool, this was not my kind of party, but I couldn't back out either. I was supposed to be one of the tough guys myself. We parked, and Simon walked us through the crowd saying hello and shaking hands. Inside we went, guns, girls and all.

We found a table, sat, and ordered some drinks. TC and I danced for a couple of songs, and as we returned to our seats, Simon asked me, "Mono wanna meet el patron?"

Meeting Pablo could go so many ways. None looked good. *Is he setting a trap for me? Are they testing me? If I say "yes"...*

"No thanks, there is too much heat right now...if something happens...I don't want to be blamed." *Besides, Pablo might want a piece of TC.*

He smiled. "Sure..." He was short and stocky, could pass for a Samoan, his front separated teeth made his smile look like he was about to bite someone, or like he had heartburn.

"Thanks anyway…" I patted his back smiling back.

I felt Pablo's presence in the darkened club. For all I knew, he might have been seating behind me listening to our exchange. My heart raced and I tried not to look around. I guessed he was making his rounds, visiting tables in the shadows.

We got out of there undamaged by heat exposure and, apparently, with a pass from the big boss.

The warning came a few days later.

We were at Aquarius, another restaurant-nightclub, with Simon. The waiter came to the table and spoke to Simon on hushed tones. I couldn't hear. Simon pulled his gun from the waistband and gave it to the waiter. He nodded towards me and said. "You should give him your piece too. The police raided the parking lot and they'll come inside soon." I took my jacket off, unclasped the shoulder holster, and passed it to him reluctantly.

The waiter waved us to follow. Simon stood pulling his girlfriend with him, and I followed with TC in tow. We got behind the bar, and the bartender opened a low door hidden on the mirrored wall. We crouched to pass, and found ourselves on the darkened restaurant, which was already closed. We stood in the shadows overlooking the parking lot with two other couples.

Five SUV Patrols blocked the exits of the parking lot, and as policemen searched a couple of cars and questioned the occupants, others came up the stairs and entered the nightclub.

We watched silently.

After a few minutes, the cops went out, headed down to the SUVs, and left.

We waited in the dark. Three Toyota Land Cruisers and

two Mitsubishi Monteros soon pulled into the parking lot, bringing us back to attention. A group of heavily armed men spilled out of the luxurious vehicles. The new arrivals dressed in civilian clothing but had the attitude and weapons of law enforcement.

I nodded towards the parking lot. "What's up?"

Simon shook his head. "Don't know…"

Were these DAS agents, *Colombia's FBI, or the F2,* undercover police? I feared them more than the *sicarios,* the Cartel's killers. People detained often disappeared, or were found raped and tortured.

One of the new arrivals climbed up the side stairs towards the restaurant, entered, then walked toward us. "Hey Simon, what's up?" He shook his hand, then came to me, patted my back and shook my hand. "Mono, the *Doctor* sends his greetings and congratulations for a job well done."

A chill shot down my spine. "Thanks."

He turned around and went back the way he'd come, got in one SUV followed by his men and the caravan drove into the night.

I started breathing again, and then turned to Simon. "Who was *that?"*

He gave me a half cocked smile. "Pablo's head enforcer."

I shook my head. "But, how did he know…?"

"Let's go party." Simon said and walked back to the disco.

This was worse than the "eye in the sky" feeling.

TC kept her cool. I wondered if the gravity of the situation had registered in her mind. She didn't ask anything, just followed Simon, swaying, silky blond hair flowing, and high hills clicking.

We partied all night, got up early in the afternoon, and got ready to go for dinner. Jumping in the Jeep, we drove on the *Autopista*, the road by the side of the Medellín River. As I took the exit to get into Avenue 33, I noticed a Mitsubishi Montero, on front of us, screeching to a stop, backing-up rapidly, and then getting behind us on the ramp. I stepped on the gas and the big V8 engine roared, its power pushing us against the seat. Counting on the roundabout intersection's small police post to be manned, I rushed there.

The officers had spread out, assault rifles ready, as they saw the Jeep coming at high speed. We screeched to a halt, and I jumped out of the Jeep.

One cop pointed his assault rifle at my chest and yelled. "Stop! What's going on?"

I halted and TC scurried behind me. I looked over my shoulder into her terrified eyes. "Don't worry. It's going to be okay" Sometimes she looked as a hardened woman, sometimes a helpless girl. It came handy. What a duo. I acted and she played her part.

They surrounded us. The officer in charge calmed down when he heard me speaking English, and got busy staring at TC's legs.

"They want to steal our car." With wide eyes, I pointed at the car now stopping behind mine.

Four men holding machine guns jumped out of the red Montero and rushed toward us. The cops didn't flinch.

This couldn't be good. They were DAS, the most feared of

all Colombian's law enforcement agencies. These hardened agents used all means to prove their suspicions.

The agent in charge identified himself, leveled a scowling gaze at me, and asked me. "Where were you going?"

I looked into the eyes of a killer and my blood turned into ice. "Going out to dinner." TC clung to my arm and I looked at her, offering more confidence than I felt. "Don't worry, it's going to be fine, babe."

"Where are you coming from?"

"Envigado. I'm staying at my sister's apartment. We're from California." I pulled my wallet, and gave him my driver's license and the Jeep's registration.

He inspected the documents. "What do you do for living?"

"I am a jewelry designer, mostly custom jewelry - silver and onyx, things like that." My strategy was to give him extra details to distract him.

"We have information about a Jeep like yours leaving the scene of the bombing of a pharmacy in Envigado this morning." His voice as cold as ice, and his eyes burned the back of my skull.

"I wouldn't be driving my girlfriend to dinner in the same car I rode to plant a bomb this morning…that would be stupid." How insulting. Gulping, I realized I had been too rough with my answer.

I translated to TC and she shuddered.

He held my gaze. "Follow us to the station."

I fought not to show my fear. If they found the revolver inside the center console of the Jeep, the permit I had wouldn't pass their scrutiny. Simon had gotten me the permit, and the gun. *Did Simon get me a hot gun?* A regular road block officer wouldn't catch the fake military official's signature, but these guys would, and they would torture me...not to mention what they would do to TC. They drooled. In my mind's eye, I saw a darkened basement, electrocution equipment, knives, drills, and a line of men...

I walked on shaky legs, opened the Jeep's door for TC, went around and got in the driver's seat. As we followed them, I looked for opportunities to get rid of the gun. The center console wasn't secured to the floor of the Jeep. It fit snugly between the custom leather seats. So I got an idea, and told TC to get ready to get out of the car at my signal.

As we approached a corner, and the agents' car signaled to turn, I slowed down, and the red light gave me the opportunity we waited for.

I stopped. "Now. Get out!" We jumped out of the Jeep, and with the console under my arm, I waved a taxi to stop. Opening the taxi's door for TC, I shoved the console on her lap.

"I love you babe, be careful." Then added without much conviction, "I will be okay."

Blue eyes shadowed by terror, she whispered, "I love you too."

I gave the driver twenty dollars and the address of the apartment, then bolted back to the Jeep as the red light changed.

I turned the corner and one of the agents, now on foot, gestured me to stop. He pointed at a parking place. They didn't seem to notice that TC was gone.

The agent waved me in and I followed him inside the old house. I stared at the back of his head and walked down the darkened corridor. An ice block filled my stomach. *How many didn't make it out of here…I'd rather be with Pablo's enforcers.*

The house served as headquarters and had a central patio surrounded by rooms converted into offices. He led me into one and told me to sit. The near-empty desk was occupied by another agent busy looking at a computer screen. The Jeep's registration was on the desk.

"Your car is stolen." He said without looking at me, and kept typing.

"I bought it at a dealership in El Poblado."

"They steal them in Venezuela and bring them here for sale." He gave me a blank stare.

I shrugged. "I have no idea what you are talking about, may I call the dealership?" I was relieved the interrogation had shifted from the bombing to the Jeep. I doubted they torture me for that.

"Go ahead." He still studied the computer screen. "Use that phone over there." He pointed at a desk in the corner of the room.

I called the dealership and told the owner of the problem. I was relieved that they were still there. I had bought the car on a previous trip, had it rebuilt and painted, which didn't help. In Colombia, painting a car a different color required more paperwork than buying it. Now, the small dealership gave me no confidence, in the light of the situation. Come to think of it, it looked like the perfect front for the kind of operation the agent was describing. The owner asked me the name of the officer in charge and told me he'd take care of the issue.

After two hours of phone calls and questions, I finally got back in the Jeep and headed back home. TC was pretty shaken, so we went for a late dinner, and life went on.

The bombing had been a couple of blocks from our apartment, but we'd got used to hear the bombs and guns going off, we didn't even notice. In California, I didn't carry a gun, nor did I have to prove I was one of the bad boys. But now, all these blasts, raids, and bandido intrigue, got on my nerves. I needed to get out from under that evil blanket. We needed sunshine.

We packed and drove to the north coast of Colombia, a gorgeous, tropical, and exotic vacation area.

The ten hour drive was a total adventure. We crossed several small towns where police, customs, and army, sat up individual check points. We were stopped, questioned, checked for proper documentation, and searched by each group.

At one of the stops, the cop asked if the cats were wild, the long haired poor things panted inside their cages in the heat of the afternoon. They were black Persian cats, and Diablo was a big boy, it didn't look friendly.

After a couple of the stops, I discovered that putting a few bills under the driver's license gave us a quick pass without the search and the two-hundred questions game.

We stayed in Cartagena for a couple of days, then went to Santa Marta and settled in an apartment on *El Rodadero*, the nicer part of town. My sister got us a bargain through a friend. The apartment was a block from the beach and near the main street, a perfect spot to relax.

The only cares were the money transfers from the bank in Medellín to our little paradise. The bureaucracy and red tape made me wish I had my guns.

A hurricane came and went. We partied and enjoyed the change of atmosphere.

After the storm, we went to isolated beaches, ate fresh fish, and relaxed under the palm trees. At one of our outings, TC got eaten by mosquitoes, and I had to take her to the doctor for treatment, but after a few days of TLC, we went on having a good time. Like everything else, it got old.

Restless, the partying got dull, and I saw the futility of it all. No purpose, no direction, no satisfaction. I tried to fill the emptiness with sex, alcohol and drugs. Hiding in paradise, hiding from myself, but, where I went, there I was.

The hot tourist season came, and the rent went up. The owner could charge for a week what we'd been paying for the month. After nearly three months, we packed and went back to Medellín.

I spent a couple of weeks establishing new connections, and making sure there were no hard feelings with old ones. Then, it was time to return to the U.S. Besides, the ambience was too hot, bombings and killings every day. The rumors were that Pablo had executed a couple of his partners over an accounting issue. I'd had enough of this cemetery cruising, and we flew back to sunny California.

11 THE SPIRITUAL DARKNESS

We rented a home in Laguna Hills and decided to take a brake from party. But TC kept going strong, like the Energizer bunny, going on and on and on. This woman could party. It didn't end well.

TC left on vacation, a weekend with a girlfriend in Santa Barbara. When she got back, I found a motel receipt on top of the bathroom counter. I called the motel and told the clerk my sister was missing, the last time I known from her, she'd called from the room there. He wouldn't give me any information until I threatened to call the police. Then he told me that they -the brunette and the blond- had been partying all weekend with all kinds of guys coming in and out of their room.

Betrayed, I kept the information for myself. I brewed a bitter pot that boiled over at the wrong time.

One night after Sushi, beer, and sake, she told me she was going to drop me off then go to the convenience store to get cigarettes. I knew she had some left, and got suspicious. I didn't have phone service at home so I wouldn't be tempted to answer a business call-a page- from where I lived. I figured she went to make a call, to whom, I didn't know.

At some point, while waiting for her to return, I blacked out. When I woke up the next day, vomit covered the floor next to the bed, and I was dressed in my late-night-bandido custom, black leather pants, black silk shirt, gloves, and a long leather coat.

My eyes scanned the room, landing on the MAC-10 laying on the bed. A line of bullet holes stretched across the wall. I staggered to the door of the bedroom. One of the bullets had gone through the wall and cracked the mirrored door of the walk-in closet.

TC was gone, nowhere to be found.

I made some phone calls and found her at her sister's house in Los Angeles. She told me I'd shot at her and chased her out of the house, but the machine gun had jammed. I'd tried to unblock it while standing in the driveway. All the while, she'd run and hid under a neighbor's car until I went back into the house, and then she'd left for her sister's.

I said I didn't believe her, and she told me to go and check the driveway. I did, and at least ten bullets peppered the ground.

Though she came back for a while, living *La Vida Loca* came to an end, and we parted as friends. She returned to Santa Cruz and came to visit a couple of times with her girlfriends.

Waiting for the new connections to come through, I tried to make a living making jewelry. I worked mainly with silver and onyx, and sold my pieces to shops at the Fashion Island Mall in Newport Beach.

I couldn't design under pressure, or that is what I believed, besides I wasn't used to working for a living. Those idle months waiting for the loads had made me lose the order of things. I didn't know what a real job was. So in an attempt to get my life straight, I took a job in Neiman Marcus Department Store, working at the custom jewelry department. Their lines were gorgeous. I offered advice on the pieces that would look good with clothing, hair style and color, or face shape and complexion. Women loved the attention.

It was a good time in my life. I could barely cover the bills but I was happy and somehow in tune with my inner-self. An artist at heart, I created and found harmony, something missing while wheeling and dealing. My spirit torn between the two identities, but, being a good boy I was making no money. So I kept pressing forward on my connections making phone calls to the people in Colombia.

After nearly a year of working at the mall, I got some action. I received twenty kilos but I had no clients, so I got busy freebasing. Gil had taught me to cook the cocaine back to base, and I smoked for days. Needless to say my straight job days were over.

During this time, I went to a bookstore and found a book about Magic on the New Age shelves. I took it home and settled by the fireplace with my black cats around me. By now Diablo had three litters with Angel. I kept one of each litter, Natas, Isis, and Monster.

The book contained a ritual in Latin. As I read it aloud a presence filled the room. Three questions came into my mind and I answered, "Yes."

The darkest time of my life started that night in Laguna Hills, California. Smoking crack and practicing black magic.

A couple of days later, I went to my favorite Sushi restaurant by the Dana Point Harbor and ordered beer and sake. A tall man dressed in black sat beside me, and as we started talking and I noticed that his ring had a pentagram. I asked him about it, and he responded with the same three questions. "Are you ready? Would you follow him? Would you give him you soul?" I said, "Yes." And I got my confirmation.

I gave Satan my soul.

My house had three bedrooms and I dedicated one to the Magic practice. I covered the walls and window with black fabric, made an altar put in my favorite chair – shaped like an elephant and made of one piece of wood - and enclosed the altar and the chair within a circle made of a strand of natural fabric laid on the carpet.

The altar had each of the four elements represented by a glass of water (water), a rock (earth), a feather (air), and a candle (fire). I added two tall candle holders on the sides, a sheet of copper with the pentagram cut-out, a solid silver fork with Hebrew engravings I'd copied from the book, a wand - of wood from a special tree - with silver tips, and a wood plate for the offerings.

I memorized the ritual in Latin and practiced continually. Got more books, and got deeper and deeper in it. This spirit world presented a dangerous and thrilling path to play in, it made me feel powerful and in control of my destiny.

I designed a gold and silver ring with the pentagram in the center and the elements' symbols engraved on the sides. It was a dramatic looking piece of jewelry and through it attracted many to that world.

Rituals brought money, sex, and power. Manifestations abounded, and practicing continued. Darkness surrounded me and Satan's presence followed me.

My wardrobe consisted solely of black or white clothing.

Usually I freebased for two or three days, slept a day, and

then got up vowing never to smoke again. All the Black Label whiskey left my stomach raw, so I often went to a local seafood restaurant for some fish soup, had a beer while waiting for the food to come, then some more beers. Half drunk again, and the vow out of the window, I repeated the cycle.

The highs turned me into a paranoid monster. To keep my hair from burning with the pipe, I wrapped a bandana around my head. Then I put on my military jacket and sat on the floor surrounded by the machine gun, the pistol, clips filled with enough bullets to carry a week's battle, and binoculars. I saw people in the field behind the house, the hallucinations kept me glued to the window.

Going to the bathroom brought this weird guy to the mirror. I squinted and turned sideways looking at the apparition. He sounded like me, but didn't look like me anymore, I looked like a skinny teenager and my skin had turned grey.

One of those nights, I was drying the crack on a sheet of newspaper and the paper started to undulate. I was so high I though it was kind of fun, until a light started to fly around the room. I got my ring out of the drawer and put it on. I could feel a presence. A cold wind shifted around me and made my hair stand. The light went away after I conjured his name. Then, there was a knock on the door of the bedroom. I froze, this was more than I had bargained for, but the crack had created a path and I couldn't close it.

In the book, at the beginning of the ritual, there were four invocations to be made at the four cardinal points of the circle, four names is Hebrew.

I walked to the door and stood there. My heart pumped in my ears, sweating and shaking, I made my favorite invocation –

Yodh-Heh-Vahv-Heh guard me and protect me - and opened. Two hoof prints indented the carpet. At that time, I didn't know what the names meant, but later I found out. They were the Tetragrammaton, the four Hebrew letters usually transliterated YHVH or JHVH, for Yahweh. I was glad that God had been with me the whole time.

That experience didn't stop me from continuing to practice, au contraire, pushed me further in. I believed I had God's protection and Satan's power.

How stupid.

I finally got a client for the twenty kilos stashed under my bed. My cousin Tomas made the connection and gave me the number to deliver the money - 120 grand.

I made contact. The guy told me to bring the money to the Long Beach Airport area, and to call his beeper when I got there, pretty much standard procedure.

I packed the money in a shoe box and wrapped it as a present. It was Christmas Eve. When I got to the area, stopped at a supermarket, and called from the payphone by the front door. After several minutes, he hadn't returned my call. A knot formed in my stomach as I looked around at the crowded parking lot. The phone rang just as I was about to leave. I answered and he asked me where I was. He told me to wait for him to call back. I heard other people and beepers going off, then him talking with someone else in the background.

Something was seriously wrong.

I was breaking my modus operandy. I'd lowered my guard and didn't leave at the first sign. Now, it was too late.

A police cruiser drove into the parking lot. I started to walk towards my Chevy Blazer watching the patrol car out of the corner of my eye. My black SUV with big tires wasn't exactly a stealth vehicle. I got in and started to drive away. The block of ice in my stomach sent a chill to the back of my skull.

I pulled out of the parking lot and headed towards the 405 Freeway. I almost made it. The police patrol got behind me and turned on its lights. I pulled over right on the freeway overpass.

The officer came to the window. "Good night, I'm stopping you for the tinted windows, they're illegal."

"No, the back tint is from the factory. My understanding is that tinting the front is illegal, these aren't." I pointed to the right front window.

He pointed to the sidewalk. "Please step out of the car."

I got off, and stood between my truck and the patrol behind it.

Another cruiser, this one a K-9 unit, stopped behind the first one and the officer brought his dog by my side. The huge German shepherd growled and barked as if it felt the evil within me. I looked at it, whispered my invocation, and yelled, "Shut up!" and it did. The officer frowned, looked at his dog, and then at me.

A small crowd gathered at the other side of the overpass watching the action.

Two vice cops parked behind the K-9 patrol, walked to the front of my Chevy, and greeted the officer. One asked me, "May we search your car?"

"No"

"Why not?"

"Why should I agree...you still gonna do it anyway." I shrugged.

They searched, brought the box, put it on the hood of the police cruiser and opened it.

The crowd grew, and cars passing by slowed down and the passengers stared. I was embarrassed.

The detective in charge waved the money, "Is it yours?"

"No, that is not even my car."

"Whose is it?

"A friend of mine."

"So you don't know what this is."

"It looked like a Christmas present."

"Is this yours?"

"My savings, shipping them to my country..." I stared at his eyes as if it made it more believable.

He stared back, "If you say that it is yours, you are going in with it."

"And if I say it isn't, you let me go?" It was going to be a dark Christmas anyway.

"Yes."

"Then, it's not mine."

He waved me away. "Go."

I walked to my car on shaky legs, got in, and drove into the

405 Freeway South. I couldn't believe they had let me go.

The next day I called Tomas from a payphone. "It was a set-up. Who gave you that number?"

"Let me call you back, I need to talk with the boss." "You gave me the number, you are responsible." I screamed.

"Mono…I call you tomorrow." He stammered.

"I am not paying the money."

"Got to talk to the boss." I cursed him and slammed the phone down.

Next day I called him. We agreed he'd cover half, and I would pay the other half with work.

The continuing months, I practiced magic for protection and prosperity. My delusions were rewarded and Satan answered my rituals almost immediately.

The New Year celebrations passed, and Spring break came, for me, with a deadly harvest.

My mother called me. "Mono, someone knocked on the front door and told me they had a delivery of flowers from you. I opened and they pushed me to the floor."

My blood turned into ice. "What do you mean, Mama?"

"They said that if you don't pay, they will come back."

"Sorry Mama, I'll take care of it, okay? It will not happen again. I promise." My brain boiled in anger.

"Mono, be careful…" She started to cry. "You can't

come..."

"Do you have my revolver? Call your sister and go to her ranch until I come."

"Mono..." She said between sobs. "Don't come, they'll kill you..."

"Mama, listen carefully. Call your sister and go to her ranch. I'll come and get you when this is over. I love you. Please do as I say, please promise me that you get out of town as soon as possible, Okay?"

"Okay...be careful..." She hanged up.

I'll kill them all! They're going to pay. But... who were they? I couldn't blast my cousin...

I called Tomas and screamed into the phone. "What the hell is going on?"

He stuttered, "Victor wants his money now."

"What does Victor have to do with this?" Victor was a pompous creep, but I didn't think he would be capable of something like this. Someone else had to have given the order to go to my mom's house.

"It's   his   money."   He   whispered.
"What is wrong with you, cousin? I am not hiding. Why did they go to my mother's house like that? You told them where she lives...you ain' right, man...all you guys had to do was to call me."

"Victor wants you to come here to talk about it...next week."

"You're kidding?"

"Next week, Mono…" He said firmly.

I cursed, "Fine, see you there…" I cursed and hanged up.

12 THE WARLOCK

I got to Colombia, went to my mom's house, and picked up my gun. I put it in my shoulder bag – a small leather satchel, similar in appearance to a saddlebag but worn over the shoulder, and used by businessmen throughout the country. Then, I contacted Victor. He was to pick me up at a bar in El Poblado the next afternoon.

I went to the bar and waited. They wouldn't kill me until the debt was cancelled, so I had a couple of tequilas and tried to relax. A Toyota pulled by the curb, Victor honked and waved. I paid the bill, went to the car, and got in the back because there was another guy with him.

These guys were another breed of *traqueteros,* drug traffickers from good families piggy-backing with the pool of investors, daddy's boys wanting to be richer.

Victor greeted me, started driving, and went on chatting with his companion about whatever…

Seated behind the other guy, I watched the backs of their heads and thought about the mess their brains would make on the SUV's windshield.

*Nobody touches mom. A*n old rule in the cartel.

The new comers were ruthless and rule less.

I stared at the back of their heads. *This other guy does not even know how close he is to ending up in a ditch with a bullet through his skull.*

My breathing became labored and I started to sweat. Opening my shoulder bag resting on my lap, I grasped the revolver's grip, a special grip I'd bought in California…The cold rubber felt good to the touch. I could shoot through the bag, but…*How many people knew they were picking me up. Were they watching my mom? Did Tomas tell them where she could be hiding?* I took my hand out of the bag and stared out of the window.

He drove to a commercial area and then into an empty warehouse. As we got out of the SUV, Victor and the other guy stood aside and behind me. A somber-looking, dark-haired man came out of the office with Tomas and two others. A chill ruffled my soul. His shoulder bag looked heavy, and it was open. Now I knew who had been to my mother's home, the enforcer. No doubt who was in charge now.

If it was Victor's money, why was this guy involved? Were they going to smoke me right there? Time seemed to slow down.

The darkened warehouse had an opening toward the back, but it was too dark to see what was there. To my right was a walk-in freezer's door, and in the corner to my left, the office where they had come from. I had seen a "Seafood something" sign above the warehouse's door, but there was no smell. It was cold.

I walked towards the enforcer, who stood with the others by the office's opened side door.

"Hi, Mono." The enforcer said as I stood about four feet away.

"How are you doing?" I nodded to him, to the rest behind him, and then slowly nodded at my cousin, staring at him a little longer.

"Mono, you have to pay the money now." The enforcer rested his hand on the opened handbag.

"You didn't have to go to my mom's house."

"We did what we had to do."

"I wasn't hiding." I pointed to Tomas with my nose, while resting my hand on my open bag also. "He had my number."

He took a step toward me. "You have to pay the 120 now."

Out the corner of my eye I saw Victor and the other guy moving behind me. *Six people and six bullets.*

"I don't have the money." I looked at Tomas. "Didn't you tell them? You have to pay half...you didn't, did you?"

"What are you talking about?" The enforcer glanced at Tomas and back at me.

"He gave me the number for the delivery, it was a set-up, he pays half...I pay sixty and he pays sixty..." I nodded to Tomas. "Right?"

The enforcer looked at Tomas and back at me again. "Okay, when can you pay?"

"I don't have the money, I'll pay with work."

His black eyes drilled me. I looked at his long dark and

fingers resting on the handbag, his gaze flicked to my hand resting on mine. I glanced at the other men, back at him, and then stared at the floor.

How did I get involved with these guys? I just wanted to make money. I worked hard, never stole, or tried to take anybody's clients, not really. Power-plays and fear didn't mix well in my brain. I trusted my cousin, and there I was...glaring at him through slits.

Bitter, betrayed, and broke. A good time to die.

"Okay, call when you're ready..." He stepped into the office.

I got back into Victor's SUV without saying a word. Victor and his sidekick climbed in and we drove out of the dark warehouse. I stared out of the window thinking of ways to kill Victor, though he wasn't worth it. *Patience...they will get killed all by themselves...*

I flew back to California with new plans and new problems.

Evil grew within me. Black Magic promptly led me to its real purpose. It drew me deeper into darkness. I called on, and trusted Satan. I knew that path had consequences, but power and pleasure pushed me forward. Darkness surrounded me, and closed its grip in my heart like a steel vise increasing the strength of the enemy within exponentially. Evil, by nature, couldn't bring anything good. Satan's power could only bring destruction and misery. But, my polluted mind sang... *you are doing just fine Jack*...a deadly tune.

Nevertheless, I pushed forward, read more books, made more tools, bought more artifacts, and practiced, practiced, practiced, and reaped the results. I *had the power* to make things happen. Rituals for money brought business, rituals for women brought knocks on my door shortly after. I only lacked a soul and satisfaction. The hole inside me swallowed everything. Evil harvest, fun for a moment, brought a disastrous reaping, living with the consequences for the rest of my life, but worse, others reaped similar results because of my influence.

I ignored the warning signs. The Long Beach encounter with the law didn't register into my clouded world of fantasy. I continued to do small jobs and party in between.

Even though *"good"* things appeared to be happening, the signs of a horrible ending were also present. Delusion, Satan's foundation.

Visualization was a big part of my magic practice. I saw what I *wanted* to see or make happen. Kind of a claim it and gain it type of philosophy. Gloom prevailed because of my choices.

Reaping time came in late October.

I drove out of the Laguna Hills home, the sun shinning high in the late morning. A police helicopter flew by as I stopped at the intersection of Moulton Parkway and La Paz road. I thought about the MAC-10 under my pillow, how I should give it to Crystal for safe keeping. Though she'd reacted badly to her initiation to the master, she continued to hang around and was easily influenced.

I drove to Costa Mesa to meet a Colombian friend who wanted me to design jewelry for his wife with some emeralds he'd stored in a safety deposit box. We went to his bank in Garden Grove and while I waited for him outside, the helicopter flew overhead again.

The thought about the Mac kept nagging me. He came out of the bank and I took him to get his car at a friend's detailing business, agreed to meet at my house, and drove away.

Driving south on the 405 Freeway as I approached La Paz exit, the song on the radio had me going. Keeping the speed along with the beat of the song, I decided to get off on the next exit.

I took the Oso Parkway exit and as I turned on Cabot road, the helicopter zoomed over the hill. Then, it was too late.

I didn't even see the police cruiser get behind me, lights on, the officer sounded the siren, "Pull over, now." The cruiser's PA system startled me.

A familiar feeling iced my stomach. I'd these kinds of premonitions since I was a teen, and I'd *learned* to pay attention to them, but here I was again. *How could I get out of this one?* I put my hope in Satan's help, a stupid kind of prayer, but it had worked before though…

I pulled over. Invoking the dark powers from within gave me a sense of comfort but it quickly dissipated as the situation evolved. Keeping my eyes closed didn't stop reality from opening them for me.

The policeman came to my window. "I'm stopping you for tinted windows, may I see your driver's license and registration, please?"

I looked at him, a mocking smile on my lips. "The back tint is factory's…I understand that only the front windows should *not* be tinted" An old script…*Did they learn that line in the police academy?*

Red faced, the veins in his thick neck about to pop out, and his blue eyes glowing. He growled. "License and registration, please."

Something inside me stirred, and the little wisdom I had left told me to shut up. I gave him the documents.

"Please step out of the car, and stand over there." He pointed to the curb.

Two cars parked behind his cruiser and four detectives came around.

The agent in charge spoke up. "May we search your car?"

"Go ahead." *Maybe I'd get out of this one...there's nothing incriminating in the truck, is there...?*

They jumped at it like kids on an Easter hunt. One of them took the truck's keys out of the ignition, whispered something to the agent in charge, and drove away with his partner.

My interrogator held my driver license. "Where do you live, Jack?"

"It's right there on the license..."

He pretended to read it one more time. "Yes, it's a street address, but we know it's a P.O. box..."

I never listed my home address for the driver's license or car's registration, instead, rented post office boxes that had a street address for that purpose.

I looked into the agent's cold eyes. "Oh...well..." *This was not good...They already knew...*

They continued searching the truck. After a while, the detective that had taken the keys returned, and said something to the one in charge.

"Take us to your house. Go ahead, we'll follow." He gave

me the truck's keys.

"Why?"

"Because I say so…" He pointed to my truck. "Go."

My mouth went dry. *I'm gone!* All hope fled. *How much time would I do for the machine gun and the silencer?*

I figured they had tried to get in the house with the keys but the only way in was the garage opener. I had all the windows sealed with screws and safety locks. *If I make them get a search warrant is going to be worse…*

I got in the truck, and they followed me.

My Colombian friend, pale and wide-eyed, waited with another detective on the sidewalk.

I parked on the driveway, and opened the garage door.

Cars came from all directions, parked, and a whole troop of detectives stormed in and searched. Two agents took my friend to the kitchen, questioned him, and took his picture.

A policeman escorted me inside and ordered me to sit on the living-room couch. *I hope they don't search the couch…*I had another identity's driver's license and Social Security hidden in a fold of the leather.

As they went through the house, one detective tried to open the room for the satanic practice. It was locked. He tried the keys on my keychain, opened the door and entered the darkened room. Spooked, he backed out. His head spun toward me. "What the hell is that?"

I looked at him and shrugged.

The search continued.

I heard a shout of victory. A tall blond with closed chopped hair came out of my bedroom with a little bag of light brown powder. Beaming, he chuckled, and waved it in front of me. "What do we have here, Jack?"

"Mother-of-Pearl powder, applied with cream helps to erase scars."

"Sure it does." Another detective brought a test tube with a white liquid. He poured a bit of powder in the tube, capped it, and shook it. The liquid didn't change color. It wasn't cocaine or crack.

I smiled.

He frowned.

They resumed their search with vigor.

It was then that the real victory came. A stocky Latino came out of my room holding in one hand my precious MAC-10 with the silencer attached, and in the other hand, the semi-automatic pistol. A following agent carried the high capacity magazines –three for each weapon. "He's ready for war!" He beamed.

They all smiled.

I stared at the floor.

"We got "the Man with the Thousand Faces." The leader reported on the radio.

The officer guarding me said. "Get up." Smirking in my face, he snapped one handcuff, turned me around, and cuffed the other hand behind my back. "You're gone, *Jack*." He pushed me towards the door.

I looked at my friend's soiled pants and into his eyes. *If you gave me away...*

The uniformed officer escorted me outside and into the police cruiser. They finished searching the house. One agent carried out a box full of pagers and cell phones.

Who had ratted? My friend? One of my girlfriends? I had been hanging around at a Sushi bar in Lake Forest and those guys were into guns and all kind of mischief. I wouldn't be surprised if the heat had come from them.

As I sat in the cruiser, the stocky detective came out of the house and played with my *Muda,* or Maggy, –the MAC-10- my baby and precious party companion. He pretended he was in a shootout, crouching, he waved it around. I could see the magazine still attached and hoped he hadn't taken the bullet out of the chamber. The trigger was very sensitive, fully automatic, at an advertised 700 rounds per minute, my ride would be cheese before he knew it.

Pull the trigger...please.

Maggy and *la Chiquita,* the little one, a Smith & Wesson 9 mm semi-automatic pistol, were my last party companions left. Now they were gone too. *What kind of life is this? My only "friends" are tools of death. How did I get here? What's the purpose of all this?*

I spent three days in jail. My friend got me out on bail.

My attorney's strategy was that the detectives didn't have a warrant for the search. The deal he got for me included to plea guilty to the removal of the serial number of the machinegun - which I didn't know had been removed - paid twenty five dollars fine, and time served - the three days in jail.

Two months later, assault weapons were banned in the State of California by the Roberti-Roos Assault Weapons Control Act of 1989. Then, the sentence would had been years, not days.

I didn't pay attention to that warning, and after one of my money rituals I decided to knock on old doors.

Simon got me picking up money for a while. It was a hotter branch of the business. I felt the danger closing in, and after a couple of contacts went down, I stopped.

According to Simon, there was a project starting in Texas. So I packed my Suburban, hooked a trailer with my Corvette, packed a couple of bags, and went to Houston. I asked one of my sisters to come from Colombia to stay with me for a while. It was important that the neighbors saw a couple living in the house. We leased a one story home in Houston and settled to wait. It took a while.

I dedicated a room in the house for my satanic practices. I called upon Satan and he answered in his own crafty ways. Once I opened that door, it cost me. I received all I asked for, but the emptiness inside increased exponentially. I sought to fill the hole inside just to find it getting bigger. I became a miserable puppet in fancy clothing.

Texas wasn't my territory and I didn't feel as confident there. We waited, partied, traveled around, and spent money.

Six months passed. Finally I got the phone call and went to a lunch meeting. My sister was to get out of the house and wait for my call. If I received the load, she was to go to a hotel and stay there until the end of the operation. At the meeting, my contact told me that there was not going to be a delivery, so I excused myself, went to the payphone at the back of the restaurant, called my sister, and told her to go home.

A couple of days later, we had to do the same, but that time I got the load. It took a couple of days to prepare the delivery. Repacked the merchandize as instructed by Simon, made contact, and passed the shipment. Basically my job was to change packaging to protect the shipping method.

After all the months waiting, broke and stressed, I called Simon for my money. He said to call the person I had delivered to, but he didn't answer. I called Simon again, and he said to wait a couple of weeks, or go to Florida and get paid there.

My sister and I took turns driving, got to Miami, rested in a hotel, and the next day decided to go down to Key West, until I could arrange the cash pick up. A couple more days passed and nothing happened, so I called Simon. The people I had delivered to in Texas had gotten busted making a delivery.

Regardless, I needed my money, go back and close the Texas' house, and flee to California. He arranged for the payment, and with the cash, we got on the road back to Texas.

It was late evening when we got out of the Miami area. My sister drove while I got in the back of the Suburban, took out the speaker behind the passenger's door and stashed the money, then went to sleep. She was supposed to drive north on the 95 freeway and take the Interstate 10 west, but instead, she continued driving north into Georgia.

I woke up and asked her where we were. I looked at the map, and turned around, adding about an hour to our trip. We finally got to the I-10 west and I continued driving, as she slept in the back.

We entered Mississippi and I was getting tired. A car fell in behind us and I slowed down. As it started to pass, and as I looked to the side, I recognized that it was a trooper. Instinctively, I stepped on the brake and he continued forward a little bit. Then, he slowed down, got behind me, and turned his lights on signaling me to pull over.

This was getting old. My nerves were raw. I shivered.

The trooper came to the window and blinded me with his flashlight. "Good morning Sir, you have a headlight out." He shone the light inside. "Traveling alone?"

I looked up to the huge officer. "No, my sister is back there." I turned and pointed at her.

"That one?" He illuminated her face, and up and down her body.

"Yeah." He annoyed me.

"License and registration," he said pleasantly.

My sister stirred and sat up. "What's up?"

"Police, we have a headlight out." I reached into the glove compartment for the registration.

"Hummmm…" She rubbed her eyes.

I gave the documents to the officer.

"Texas plates, what are you doing this way?"

"We're on vacation, showing my sister Key West."

"Step out of the car and stand behind it, please."

"Sure." I opened the door. "May I check the light?" I pointed to the front.

He walked towards the front and I followed him, stepped

around him, and bumped the headlight with my fist. It went back on. "There you go, probably a bad contact."

"Yes, step behind the truck." He pointed to the back, and I followed him.

At two in the morning, wearing shorts, I shuddered, half from fear. So I got closer to the cruiser's grill to warm up.

The other officer – a young, tall redhead, with a military haircut - walked around the Chevy Suburban banging on the sides with his fist. He started on the back right side, "bang" up over the wheel, "bang, bang," and continued at the same height, "bang, bang, bang."

I held my breath and looked the other way.

"Bang, bang, bang," right over where the money was, six inches lower, it would have been a "Thud, thud, thud." Jackpot!

He banged on the doors and fender.

I breathed again.

He went around the big truck, banging away, I couldn't care less, but then, he opened the back gate, "bang, thud, bang, thud." I frowned.

"What's in there?" He pointed at the bulk over the door, and looked at the older officer standing by my side.

"The rear AC. You can turn it on if you want, it works." I said a little too soon. My sister turned wide eyes at me from the back seat. I blinked and look down, wishing she looked away.

The young trooper looked at me through slits. "I'm gonna get a screw-driver." He walked to the back of the cruiser.

I shivered. *If he starts to take panels out, the speakers are next...*"So cold...may I lean on your car, Sir?"

"Go ahead." The thick-necked officer handed me the documents as he spoke on the radio.

The radio conversation seemed far away. I understood bits and pieces. A part of my brain disconnected from the scene, and I tried to control the shaking on my legs by pressing them against the bumper of the cruiser.

The younger officer came back holding a screwdriver. "I'm gonna take that panel out..." He pointed at the AC unit, and looked at me.

I looked away, but watched him out of the corner of my eye as he started with a screw. I could feel his eyes drilling on my ear.

The radio barked something and the officer 10-4ed. "Come on. Let's go...It's getting late." The bull waved the youngster to get in the cruiser.

I closed the rear gate and got in the truck. My hands shook as I started it. I drove slowly letting them get ahead. "That was close..."

"Yes, what..." She cursed them.

"They're doing their job. We shouldn't be driving loaded this late. Besides I fitted the profile of a mule - a young Latino in a late model SUV, alone."

"I was here..." She countered.

"Yes, but they couldn't see you. Go back to sleep." I growled.

I watched the cruiser disappear. At the next town, we got a

motel room and went to sleep. The next day, we drove to Houston. After resting, I rented a truck and a trailer. We packed the few pieces of furniture I had bought there, put the Corvette on the trailer, and my sister followed in the Suburban.

13 THE TRIP TO THE GRAVE

Back in California, I closed the house in Laguna Hills, and moved to Mission Viejo. My sister enrolled to study design, and I took sculpture and film production classes.

After a few months, Simon *invited* me to Medellín to talk about the Texas operation. An invitation I couldn't refuse. I packed my bags, did a few rituals for protection, and flew south with a bad premonition.

In Colombia, stressed out, I tried to party, feeling empty, anxious, and bitter, I couldn't even have fun anymore. Before leaving, my sister had told me, "Mono, you have everything, and you are the most miserable person I know." I tried to smile as my heart ripped. She was right. Jack had disappeared under the piles of aliases, identities, and rituals. I had lost my soul. Now, what did I have to lose? This meeting could be my last one. I had pushed it too far, so far that I had no clear purpose for my life.

This is the end of the road for me, they are going to kill me, I am out of luck and there is no way I am going to risk another visit to mom's house. These guys, surely, won't deliver roses...

The night before the meeting, I partied, restless, and with a sense of foreboding that no drink could appease. Cursed, I couldn't get drunk.

I went with Simon to a hip bar. One of my favorite cousins was there, so I sat with her at a table, leaving Simon at the bar. We had a few drinks, and danced. Later, a couple of shady characters showed up and hanged out with Simon. My stomach dipped, and the hairs on the back of my neck stood on end when I saw them. They looked like sicarios - hit men. We did a couple of lines in the bathroom as I pretended to blend. But, not wanting to risk my cousin's safety, I slipped out and left. If they were there for me, they would leave her alone. If I stayed, she may get caught in the crossfire. She was at the wrong place at the wrong time with the wrong cousin. I felt death walking behind me.

I went back to the apartment my older sister had rented for me, and went to bed. The sleepless night crowded with my master's lies. I tried relaxing exercises, meditation, and positive visualizations but my mind kept creeping back to visions of three bullets hitting my chest. So, exhausted, I received them, cherished those bullets ripping me inside, then visualized them coming out reversing their action. How foolish.

A loud noise startled me awake. I crawled to the window and peered through the blinds. Under the late morning's sun, at least three hundred policemen paraded at the park in front of the apartment. There was some kind of ceremony happening. *Thanks sis, this was the perfect hideout.* I got dressed quickly and ran out the back door. I had lunch, and waited for Simon at a local bar called "Cinco Puertas", Five Doors, because it was in an old house in a corner, and had that many doors to come into the small establishment.

As I waited, a gorgeous brunette tried to park. I signaled her to back up until she fitted her vehicle in the small parking spot.

She wore riding breeches, so I asked her what kind of horse she had, and there we went flirting. We talked for a while and I asked her for dinner the next day. Tania gave me something to look forward to, if I survived.

Simon's Land Cruiser stopped in front of the bar, and waved me over. He told me where we were going and I followed him to the restaurant in my Jeep.

The meeting was at *Hato Viejo*, a restaurant in Las Palmas, a road where many unfortunate men got the *paseo*. The word meant a sight-seeing trip, but in our world, the *paseo*, consisted of the enforcers inviting the victim into their car, driving him to an isolated area, pushing him out of the car and shooting him.

Yod-He-Vaw-He guard me and protect me. I invoked as I drove into the restaurant's parking lot.

The night was beautiful, not too cold, but enough to justify the heavy jacket concealing my gun's shoulder holster. Mountain scents filled my nostrils, a refreshing rush of clean air that contrasted with the white powder my nose bled for.

As we walked, Simon said, "Did you have a good time last night?"

"Yes, I had a blast."

"I liked your girlfriend." Simon laughed.

"Hey, hands off my cousin." I forced a laugh.

"She stayed after you left." He grinned.

I looked at him, searching for a second meaning. My jaw muscle twitched. *You touch her and you're dead.*

Rage, bitterness, and frustration hit my brain. How did I get here? What was I doing with this crowd? I wanted to run away, to disappear, but I had no choice. They would kill my family. Now, to survive tonight, I had to face the boss, whoever he was.

"We share girlfriends, but not family...hands off..." I wondered if he knew of my affair with his sister. Holding the bridge of my nose, trying to relieve the building pressure, I remembered my sweet cousin's face. My one-sided rules cached up with me, and my choices were affecting innocent people.

Tense as a piano wire, I walked towards the entrance of the restaurant.

He needled, "Where did you go? I looked for you but you disappeared," his eyes seemed to look into my soul.

"My stomach," I grimaced, "something I ate...besides, you looked kind of busy. Who were those guys that came later?" *I thought you were going to get me killed. They looked like sicarios –assassins- to me.* Now it was my turn to stare at him.

"Just some guys I know..." He looked forward.

The walk seemed like a mile. *Yod-He-Vaw-He guard me and protect me....* I turned my ring's outside in, and rubbed the pentagram. The heavy ring gave me comfort.

Simon, my friend and partner in crime, led me to the sacrificial ground.

Who'll pull the trigger? How will it feel? Will they shoot me here or, take me to the car to give me the paseo? Who will decide? At least they were giving me the benefit of the doubt, a chance to clarify whatever they were thinking...

I followed Simon through the formal area of the restaurant where executives celebrated their business ventures, couples savored romantic dinners, and families gathered for anniversaries and birthdays. The restaurant had a rustic but elegant décor, a place to have a good time…not the place to die.

Simon led me to a table at the leveled terrace, by the corner.

Two men waited at the table. One of them had come to my house in California before the Texas fiasco. The other, appearing to be in charge, I'd never seen before. He looked controlled, different, educated, an intellectual behind the scenes, a "professor." The face of death. What threw me off was his carriel, the typical shoulder bag of the *Antioqueños,* the local ranchers.

We approached and I noticed they were seated against the wall. I had to sit with my back towards the room, and wouldn't see if someone approached.

Simon shook "the professor's" hand. "Hi, how are you?"

"Fine, Simon, and you?"

"Very well, thanks." Turning to the other, Simon shook his hand, "Hey Rafa, what's up?"

"Good and you?" He pointed to a seat and Simon sat.

I approached the professor and shook his hand. "How are you, sir?

"Good Mono, and you?" He didn't say his name.

"Mono", my family's nickname. An indication he knew of my family. He probably had a car full of thugs outside of my mom's house that very moment, just in case I did something stupid. His peaceful eyes disturbed me.

I forced a smile. "Good thanks, it's nice to meet you." I

moved to Rafa. "Long time no see. How have you been?"

"Good Mono, all good." Have a seat, want a beer?

"Sure, beer sounds good." I sat down and laid my hands on my lap. Rubbing the ring, I silently invoked, *Yod-He-Vaw-He, guard me and protect me,* thought I knew my life depended on my answers.

The night was young. A waiter came and we ordered drinks. After a brief silence, allowing the waiter to walk away, the professor turned to me. "We want to clarify a few things about Texas."

"Sure." My firm voice feigned a confidence I didn't feel.

"When you made the first contact in Houston and were told there would be no delivery, you got up and made a phone call."

"Yes, my sister was there, and I called to tell her to go home. She was supposed to sleep at a hotel if I got the load. Simon knows her. They probably knew were she was at that very moment. You can ask her about that night if you want." I held his stare. "I didn't want her driving around in my Corvette. She drives fast and I didn't want her to wrinkle my baby."

Simon knew my sister, because, about six months earlier, I'd asked him to arrange a meeting for her boyfriend with Pablo Escobar. She'd been dating a helicopter pilot friend of mine, and Pablo's sicarios were killing the members of the organization he was connected with. I didn't want her caught in the crossfire or tortured for information, so I called Simon and he'd set the meeting with Pablo. Her boyfriend must have said the right things since he was still around after that.

Here I was at a similar meeting.

The professor pressed on. "Why did you go to Florida after your delivery?"

"I was almost out of money, Simon told me I had to wait a week or two in Houston to get paid, or go to Miami and pick up the money there."

He looked at Simon, nodded, and then turned to Rafa. "Anything else?"

Breathing slowly to keep calm, I kept my eyes on the professor while they exchanged silent messages that decided my fate.

Rafa shrugged. "No, that's it." He looked at Simon and so did I. Simon nodded.

Was I off the hook or did all the nodding meant *kill him*? Was I going to live tomorrow? Could I blast my way out with only six bullets in my revolver?

The professor stood, walked to the low fence separating the levels of the terrace, and spoke with one of the four guys at the table. Then they stood and left.

I felt cold even with the heavy jacket. It looked like there wasn't going to be a *paseo* for me today. I watched the men filing out. How much would they have gotten paid for killing me? Were they on salary? Some killed for free, for points with the boss.

This would have been a good time to have my Mag-10 but it would've been inappropriate if I showed up all strapped.

This brush with death should have shown me I was walking in spiritual darkness, evil by my side. Moving in Satan's power closer and closer to dying by the side of the road without even the luxury of a shallow grave should have made me wonder why the sleepless, restless nights, and why when sleep came it was filled with nightmares. The most common one, I was in the middle of a shootout and the bullets of my gun dropped a few feet away making me feel powerless. The opposite of what magic practice taught. It taught *I got the power!* In reality it was Satan's power feeding the enemy within.

After the meeting I went to a bar and got drunk. Tania, my rider new friend joined me. Over the next couple of weeks, we began a hot romance, and she decided to come with me to California.

***

My life was a living Hell. Satan, my lord, kept me alive for his own purposes. My pilot's dream, stolen, the innocent and optimistic youngster, disappeared, and like a bomber, my life trailed destruction and misery.

Back in California, I needed to cool down, so I trained for a Real Estate License, and got a job at a Mortgage company. I enjoyed the change and the industry.

My new bride-to-be came to California and we married on Halloween day. Money was tight so I designed the wedding rings with big cubic zirconia instead of my diamonds. She was still happy with her fake rock. Love is blind sometimes, or for some time.

But darkness prevailed, and we plowed along through a turbulent relationship. Happy times were dimmed by my drinking and pornography addiction. Magic intrigued my new wife, but lost its luster when she found porno movies stashed in the *sacred room*. She called me a fake, and demanded I get rid of my satanic practice tools. In order bring peace I threw them away in a creek by Trabuco Canyon. I wanted to make this family work. It was my prevailing dream, to have a family.

My spiritual quest took a new face. Through a fortune-teller, I met a guy who practiced Santeria, a branch of Voodoo that comes from Africa, and into the United States mainly through Cubans and Haitians. We started with cleansing rituals, but nothing stays the same, it evolves and progress, just like any bad habit, and now, I started to play with raw evil and the power of its spirits.

The newfound *Padrino,* or godfather, instructed us into the secrets of this religion. He taught as much as we could spend on the rituals. They were not cheap. We poured thousands of dollars in *santos* - artifacts dedicated to a particular deity - that were supposed to give us access to the power of the saints.

Santeria consists of a group of spiritual entities represented by idols, a spiritual hierarchy of little gods and bigger gods, goddesses and door keepers, that required sacrifices and offerings. It is like mix of Greek Mythology, Judaism and Catholicism, with a splash of Wicca and Voodoo.

But of course, it didn't stop there. My wife thrived on it, so we kept spending and supposedly became more powerful. What a joke. The only one profiting was the godfather.

I researched and collected materials about our new religion. Later studies revealed that there was a strong Judaic influence on Santeria's practices.

My godfather prohibited me from buying books, the same ones that he sold in his *botanica*, the store he managed with his wife. They had a complete inventory of artifacts, images, herbs and tools for the spells. He told me, "this is the religion of the monkey, monkey sees, the monkey does."

"Too bad, I am not a monkey. If I cannot read about it, I am not interested in practicing it." He disagreed with my answer, but wanting the money flow to continue, he sold me the books.

Away from God, evil prevails. The Santeria practices led us to *Palo Mayombe,* a darker branch that claimed to control the spirits of the dead. We were introduced to another godfather specializing in this branch. He filled a cauldron with different kinds of wood sticks, dead insects, rodents, bats, horns, and the final touch, a human bone –I didn't ask where it came from. This combination determined the strength of the *muerto,* the spirit of the dead entrapped to serve the demands of its master.

The human element alone could run up to a thousand dollars, which was the cost of a skull or *Kriyumba,* which was what I had in my cauldron. At the initiation ceremony we sacrificed a lamb to his muerto and to mine. It was supposed to give strength to the spirit chained into the cauldron, and give me the control of it.

Again, the rituals seemed to work –business increased and enemies were appeased. Powers got conjured and continued to flow. My choices always accompanied by consequences or rewards. My marriage suffered, our fights intensified, and one time, at a ritual, my wife became possessed, her facial expression contorted making her a total estranger. Also, one night I was awaken by her screams. I was punching her on my sleep. A force possessed me. I jumped out of the bed and sat on the floor trembling. Not good for the marriage either.

The ambience at the house became heavy and Tania pressed to move, so we leased a condo in Aliso Viejo. The mortgage business slowed down after the refinance boom, so I moved into home sales, but the desire to continue the legit path withered when Simon contacted me.

About a year and a half since the Texas operation, things had cooled like an ocean breeze. Barely making ends meet, and full of smoke from all those prosperity rituals, I eagerly agreed to the new project.

14 THE END IS NEAR

Pablo Escobar, hunted by government special forces and killed, opened the business with other organizations and stopped the cartels' wars.

I received 800 kilos from a new shipper. The word was that this organization had thirty tons in Mexico and needed transporters in the U.S. I wanted to get out of the drug business, and this connection provided the opportunity. A few more tons would get me on my way.

I took the load home. No stash house, no security measures. There we were, my wife pregnant, her daughter, and me, with the load in the garage of the condo. How irresponsible.

The contract paid less than before but with the condition that I would not make any deliveries of less than fifty kilos it reduced exposure and helped me to complete the project safely and promptly. There were a few complaints about the deliveries' minimum amount, but I was able to convince Simon that this was the most secure way to do it. I had no control where the load came from, but I wanted some control over the deliveries.

In the middle of the operation, my wife had complications

with the pregnancy and her doctor ordered her to be hospitalized until the baby was ready to join this model family.

There were no major problems with the deliveries until the last fifty kilos. I had a premonition, so I called Simon and somebody else answered the page.

"Who is this?" This was a serious breach of protocol.

"It's Alberto, working with Simon now." He chirped.

"I won't talk to anyone but him. Get him on the phone." I shifted, and looked around the hospital's payphone.

"Wait, here he comes."

Another voice came on the phone, it didn't sound like Simon either. "What's up Mono?"

"Who the hell is this?"

"It's me, Mono. What's up?" The speech sounded scrambled, like through one of those devices that modifies the voice.

"You don't sound like Simon…Where did we meet?"

"In Uraba. Your dad had a plantation." He said.

"What kind of motorcycle I drove there?" I felt foolish, but I had too much responsibility. How could I pay if something happened to the load?

"A Yamaha." He sounded annoyed.

"What color?" I countered.

"Red. Are you happy now? What's wrong with you?" Simon growled.

"I need my money before I deliver the last fifty." I said with a knot in my stomach. *Something is not right.*

"Don't worry; you'll get paid with the next load." He responded too quickly.

"What if there is no *next load?*"

"There is another load ready to pick-up Mono."

"Pay me the arranged fees and I will deliver the rest, then, we talk about the next job."

"Oh, by the way, there is a change. The shipper said that because of the high volume your fee is going to be less."

My vision blurred. Breathing slow and deep I leaned my head against the wall.

"Hello, Mono? Are you there?"

"It's too late to change the fee, the job is finished. You agreed to a fee and that is what you'll pay. I will not deliver the last fifty until I get paid." I felt heat rising to my head. *If something goes wrong, how could I find him?*

He countered, "They won't pay more."

"Then you have a problem…I'll wait for the money, and when cancelled, you'll get your delivery…You can't change my fee now." I slammed the phone.

This is not happening to me. Who is this new guy answering the calls? Is he paying the new guy out of my cut? No way!

I went out of the hospital, to another payphone and called my mother. "Mom, sorry about this again, but you have to get out of the house now. Go to your sister's ranch."

"Mono, I am not going anywhere."

"Mom, this is serious. These people are very dangerous and they owe me lots of money. The mechanic-Simon's nickname when talking to her- is going to come for you...he wants to rip me off. Please do this for me. Now."

In my mind, Simon's Land Cruiser screeched to a halt in front of her house, and grenades blew the reinforced steel front door. "Mom, there is no choice here. Please get out of the house NOW. You have about fifteen minutes. Call a taxi and get to your sister's. Please."

"Okay. When can I come back?" Her subdued voice ripped my heart.

"I'll let you know...I'll call your sister. Go now, Mom. You promise?" I pleaded.

"Yes. I am leaving."

"Bye mom, sorry..."

"Bye, my love, be careful." She hung up.

I sighed and pounded a fist against the phone. *This is messed up. What am I going to do? They can't find me here but they sure can find my family...* I felt disrespected and powerless. Death danced around me. I wanted to kill, and was going to get killed if I didn't play this well. And once again, to my shame, I had compromised Mom's safety.

Calculating my mom was out of town, I called them again. Simon said that the next load was ready for pick-up, so I settled for a lower fee hoping I could salvage the situation and continue working.

At that distribution level there were rotations between groups. Whoever was ready waited the turn for the next load. I felt blacked out of the waiting list permanently and I wasn't ready for retirement yet. I felt stupid worrying about the next job when my family was about to be blown away because of me. I needed to defuse the tension and try to salvage as much as possible of my fee.

Now, the next problem was, I had to meet someone to get paid. This presented me with the most dangerous situation of my career. The philosophy of working alone proved to be a big mistake now. I had no soldiers.

Simon gave me a number to call for the payment. When I made contact, I was told to go to a restaurant by the Puente Hills Mall near Rowland Heights. I waited there vulnerable and exposed. After nearly fifteen minutes, a man in mechanic's overalls showed up and gave me a big box. Something rattled inside and it wasn't that heavy. *It could be hundreds and fifties...*I jumped in my car and drove away feeling somehow relieved, but still had a cold knot in my stomach. I took side roads, checked and double checked that I was not being followed, and finally made it home.

I opened the box and my head exploded with rage. There were not enough bundles of money to make my fee. I spilled the money on the floor and horrified saw there were bundles of ones. I counted seventy five hundred dollars.

Now, it was on.

I called Simon. "I got five thousand in ones. You think I am stupid or what? Now I only take payment from you." I cursed. "Come and give me the money yourself." The phone shook in my hand.

"I can't go there, Mono" he responded.

"I don't care, if you want the fifty kilos, *you* bring me the money. Next time you call my pager I expect a Southern California area code. You have a week." I hung up. He called four days later and I told him to wait for me in the parking lot of a restaurant on El Toro road. I drove in and he walked towards my car with a shopping bag. "Hey Mono."

"All there…?" I growled.

"Yes." He handed me the bag through the car's window.

"I call you in an hour, and tell you where the loaded car is. Keep the car." I drove away.

At home, I counted the money, loaded the boxes in one of the vans I had received the load in, and drove it to the Laguna Hills Mall. I told him where it was. The job was finished, and so was I.

Money worries assaulted me immediately. The new home was going to swallow what I had received in a blink. Where was I to get the money to pay for the house? Simon would never talk to me again.

Satan stole the victory, left me empty and miserable.

I had become my worst enemy. Growing stealthily, the monster within had broken through. What a nightmare it was to live my most desired dream.

***

After a long hospitalization waiting for the baby to mature enough to come into this world, we got a beautiful baby boy.

I continued my Real Estate charade and we moved into the new home. Money went as expected. My wife had gotten a new

Suburban, and I couldn't drive the old Cadillac in that kind of neighborhood, so we bought a brand new BMW. Furniture, swimming pool, curtains, flooring, and of course we dressed up too. I changed the zirconia on the wedding rings for real diamonds, sparkly little buggers, perfectly reflecting light in my darkened world. I had visions of success, stability, an honest living, but somehow this whirlwind kept bringing me back to believing crime was the only way I could make it. I was blinded by greed.

I built a room in one of the garages and practiced my religion.

My life felt like as if a Trojan Horse had delivered its deadly load, and I spent my time fighting my own demons. I had everything, but was going too fast to enjoy it. It was all there, all the material things I lusted for, even the family I'd always dreamed about, but I felt no satisfaction. Emptiness filled my heart, like a well-dressed zombie walking on air.

One morning, as I sat in my home office, surrounded by luxury, I prayed to one of the saints to change my life. Filled with fear of losing it all, I chose to lose my pride first. I called Simon again. He spoke as if nothing had happened, but now the fee was much lower, take it or leave it. I took it.

He promised a ten-thousand kilo contract. We went from mortal enemies to vital allies in a phone call.

Oh, how deceitful Satan can be. Somehow I wasn't surprised at the magnitude of the contract. I knew Simon was into something big, that Pablo's killing had opened new doors, and I didn't ponder the downside of those alliances.

I asked for ten thousand dollars at front, and he got them delivered. I got new pagers and cellulars, rented a condo in Aliso Viejo to keep the product, and reported to Simon that I was ready for a shipment. A couple of weeks later I got the call and I met the new transporters at a restaurant in Tustin. They were clean cut Mexicans, and looked professional. The boss was my age, fit, good looking, and elegant.

I wanted to start working again and make this project the last one. Ten thousand kilos would hit the mark. At the initial meeting, I had an electronic bug detector inside a leather daily planner resting on my lap. In the middle of the meeting, while we were eating, the detector started to vibrate. My pulse raced. Though I always spoke in code, in court the code wouldn't matter if one of the persons seated at the meeting testified.

Spooked, and trying to keep a straight face, I sought an escape route. Then, the boss reached into his pants pocket and pulled the latest cellular model. It was the first model with vibration capabilities. He spoke briefly and hung up. This was the first time the detector had been proven effective.

"You almost gave me a heart attack. My bug detector vibrated when you got the call, and I thought you were wired." I put my daily planner on top of the table and opened it.

"How does it work?"

"It picks up any signal within a certain range, and it vibrated when you got the call. It can be set to beep, vibrate, and a red light comes on when it detects a transmission." Proud of my toy, I explained all the features.

"Where did you get it?" He looked impressed.

"At a spy shop up in San Fernando Valley. Here, I'll get another one." I pushed the bug detector across the table.

"Thanks." He smiled and passed it to his silent partner.

The meeting continued uneventfully, and then we went to scout the drop place in his Range Rover. This guy rode in style and didn't look out of place. I wondered how flashy he was in his territory, but somehow felt at peace. He inspired confidence.

It surprised me that the boss accepted my advice about the drop. I guessed my toy had broken the ice. Usually the one with the load sets the rules and meeting places. I showed him a restaurant in Irvine that I confirmed as a safe place for the delivery, that way we didn't have to speak about it on the phone. It also was at a walking distance from another shopping center where I could leave my car, without risking it, in case the delivery was compromised.

A couple of days later I've got a call in my pager with his code, and time for delivery.

I was back in business. This load was different. All five hundred kilos were shaped and wrapped the same. Silver taped, the same size, and perfectly shaped bricks. To me it was an indication of same shipper and lab. This made all my skepticism disappear.

When I started in the business, innocence clouded my vision. We were a young easy-going bunch, under a charismatic boss. Evil wasn't as evident. I trusted people, thinking we all had a common purpose -get the job done and make lots of money in the process. But it turned out that there was no brotherhood. Between pats on the shoulder, and with a smile on their face, all tried to stab each other in the back. Yes, of course I *knew* that we were a criminal enterprise, but somehow I wanted to *believe* something else. I wanted to trust and love my brothers in crime. Like a romantic fool thinking that a prostitute loves him. It was all moved by emptiness, a deep desire to find true love. Money changed it all. The truth turned out to be that the same one patting my back would put a bullet in my head later. At the same time, I realized that my love for big guns was a pathetic fantasy. There would by no place to hide. When they come, they get you.

There was no common plan and there was no common future. As far as I was useful, got the job done, and they got the profits, I was in the game.

Still, many got burned, friends and foes dropped right and left. Victor, the one that ordered my mom pushed to the floor, got killed. GRIN. It paid to be patient. Stupid people got taken care of by their own stupidity. Too bad Simon had already paid him.

Sooner than I thought, fate would also take care of my worst enemy. Myself.

15 THE WARNINGS IGNORED

Too many people and too much money involved. I was lost in the game and, worst of all, I ignored the warning signs. The danger brought into my mother's life and other family members, the rip-offs, and the alarmingly increase of people involved. The more people involved increased the chances of a leak, of a rat.

On the other hand, the monster within took over, nothing left of my old self. The little slip out of my dream to be a pilot became a slide into a fantastic world with no joy and no future. I had all I wanted. Money, a beautiful wife, a sweet innocent daughter –a stepdaughter that loved me as her dad- my son, a big house and a business, but nothing brought satisfaction. It was like a curse. All shiny on the outside, all dark in the inside. It was like looking at beautiful scenery through a dirty window. I knew there was something special out there but couldn't appreciate anything.

My vision of a secured future, a vision of having financial security in a legitimate world was based on a foundation of sinking sand. Soon it would crumble as reality slammed into my life like a tidal wave. The final warnings came after I finished delivering the first one thousand kilos.

I took my wife on an enchanting late honeymoon in Maui.

We stayed at the Four Seasons Hotel. It was perfect, no drinking, no hangovers, and no major problems.

I had stopped drinking New Year's Eve, 1992. While toasting, my wife had said, "You are going to get drunk again…"

I shrugged. "Just one more."

We toasted to a better 1993 and as I reached for the bottle of Champagne again, she said, "You can't stop drinking. You always have to get drunk." Frustration filled her cup.

She was right. We had been drinking every Friday, watching TV, until I passed out, often blacked-out. But that moment I made a decision. "Okay, I am not going to drink again." And I didn't.

Now, mid 1995, we enjoyed two beautiful weeks of relaxation. We went sightseeing, watched gorgeous sunsets, and took a helicopter ride that made my soul cry for flying again. We sat in front with the pilot, and as he took off, my eyes watered with the emotions and memories. Here I was, paying for something that had been my dream. I realized how lost I was.

The vacation came to an end, like everything in this life. While at the airport, I got a page from Colombia and I paged them back from a payphone. Alberto told me that he recognized the area code because he'd been there. I told him I was on my way to California. He told me the next load was waiting for me, and then he said, "We need you there as soon as possible, you are indispensable, Mono."

That should have raised a flag for me. If I were them, at the moment of realization that "El Mono" was indispensable, I would have dispatched at least another team to be in place, which was probably what they did. His slip of the tongue should have given me a warning. Either they were pumping my ego to make time to have the other team in place, or the other team had gone down already. The bottom line, I was not indispensable. Nobody was.

The lamb ran straight to the slaughterhouse.

The next sign came when I started receiving loads from another group. Again, they were Mexicans, but this time the person I met was alone. He picked me up and started rambling about their organization, the area where they had a warehouse, and other details I didn't need to know. My first law of survival – don't know more than you need. The second –don't talk about what you know. I looked at him as if he were from outer space. I didn't want sensitive information. Worst of all, he seemed to be telling the truth. That really disturbed me. If this guy had such a big mouth, and was so careless about disclosing so much to a stranger in the business, how much did he disclosed when drinking with his buddies or with unconnected family members?

In Florida, many people got killed in the old days because they told someone, or showed someone, disclosed something, and ended up rotting along with the whole family in a stash house until the neighbors smelled the corpses.

His disclosures continued, and then he said we were bringing two hundred thousand dollars to the transporters. I smiled like a hungry wolf, and looked at him with mixed emotions. So far, nobody could prove he'd picked me up. It could be a good day's profit. Also, it could be a test, a set up.

If I had a gun…I could drop him and take the money. Then, call Colombia… "I have been waiting here for an hour and nobody showed up. What's going on?"

The quick bonus would finish the swimming pool, and buy a lot of used cars for my auto dealership, my new enterprise.

How did I get here? The question I often asked in the beginning, but by now, it only passed through my mind when facing extraordinary circumstances. I had never, ever, thought or even considered killing someone to steal their money. Criminal or not, I had been taught to work for my money, earn my keep.

But there I was, looking at this guy, probably new in the business, someone used by his bosses to see if the project made it through. The business had turned that way. The bosses just burned people trying ways to push a load across the border. I didn't expect that kind of thinking at this level though. Five hundred kilos represented too much money, at least to me it did.

I had no excuse to ignore all these flaws in procedure and safety. If my project included ten thousand kilos, I calculated, at least two more teams should be already in place, each working at least the same quantity. I couldn't blame my socio-economic status, environment, upbringing, or anyone else for the chaotic situation I had put myself in. Managing this quantity alone was way over my head, but I liked the thrill, the danger, and the too-close-to-the-edge feeling. It was a combination of fear and rage, dare and death-wish. I felt a part of a greater purpose. Truly, I was *indispensable* in my own evil scheme. I was the protagonist and antagonist of my own play. It's also called *Adolescent Invincibility Syndrome*, "it will not happen to me." But, at my age it's considered *Adult Insanity Syndrome* (AIS), or stupidity.

Now I was living up to my nickname, *El Loco,* the Mad Man.

Lost inside, I just kept on going forward. Like a train without brakes, like a plane in the dark, flying blind, no instruments, like that time flying inside a cloud in Gil's plane with the radar damaged.

Now I knew Simon was working with two different organizations for sure. At least I was not the only one blinded by greed. I had two stash houses now. He'd told me to separate the loads. The silver-taped kilos delivered to people from Cali, and the other product to people from Medellín.

The project running full throttle, I got calls to pick-up before finished delivering. I was too busy to worry, but the heat was coming.

Things got pretty hectic. Delivering 500 kilos a week kept me busy. I got lists of phone numbers for my deliveries, the first one to answer would get serviced, and down the list I went until finished.

The next couple of weeks would be a challenge like no other.

July 18th, Thursday.

I met the receivers at a restaurant in Laguna Niguel. My contact told me the dark blue van had the keys in the ashtray. I was going to load it, and call them with the place for them to pick it up.

My helper had driven me to the meeting, and we had an argument on the way over. I was upset and forgot to sweep the car for bugs. Got in, and drove towards the stash house. As I made the usual turns to make sure I wasn't followed, I noticed the police helicopter, so I continued driving around. The helicopter pursued as if attached by an invisible line. I drove north to the Orange County Airport, so the helicopter couldn't follow under the landing path.

I lost them for a while, but as I got out from under the covering of the airport's airspace, they were on top of me again. The van had to have a tracking device. I took the 405 Freeway South and took the Culver Drive exit. Then made a right turn, after a couple of more turns and not seeing any cars following, I decided to make a break for it. I breathed deeply to slow my pounding heart and be able to think clearly.

There was a two-story office building nearby surrounded by tall trees that could cover my escape. Passing the strip-mall in the corner, I drove to the condos behind it. I parked the van and ran to the path between the apartments. The helicopter flew over the trees as I flattened myself against an apartment's wall. Then, I ran to the strip-mall and got inside the office building. Upstairs, the long corridor was deserted. I walked calmly in case someone came out of one of the doors to the medical offices that lined the left wall. Looking at the parking lot through the tinted windows on the right wall, I surveyed the traffic. No police cars or any other vehicles rushed in the parking lot. It all seemed normal except for the angry purring of the helicopter circling the area.

I called and told my helper to use the service driveway behind the office building, park and call me when there.

I kept looking at the parking lot, nothing suspicious, traffic kept coming in and out, wives going to the supermarket trailing children behind, and crazies going to the liquor store. My helper called after almost twenty nerve-wrenching minutes. I ran out the side of the building as the helicopter zoomed over the trees.

Still on the phone, I shouted, "Pop the hatch door, I'm gonna jump in."

"What's going on?"

My black Lexus SUV came into view as I turned the corner, "Do it! Open it…" I sprinted toward it.

I heard the "pop" of the hatch door as I approached the SUV from behind, I opened it and jumped in. "Drive, drive, drive out of here now. The police helicopter is flying over us. Drive."

"What is happening, are you crazy?" She backed up.

"Take the freeway south." I lay on the floor and looked for the helicopter under the cover of the tinted windows.

"What's wrong with you?" She maneuvered onto the street.

The new stash house I had leased was ready to move in, but I didn't want to transfer the merchandise there, seeing it as an unnecessary risk. If I went down moving between stash houses I would have to pay for the load. So my plan was to finish delivering the merchandize I had at the Aliso Viejo condo, then start using the other place. This decision will prove to be catastrophic.

She grumbled and complained as she drove out the luxurious SUV -a common sight in that neighborhood- and a lone female at the wheel, who would suspect her? She looked like Sade, the singer, beautiful and sexy.

We drove south to San Juan Capistrano and called Simon from a gas station's payphone. "I am having problems with the last order."

"Who?"

"Enrique."

"I need new contact numbers and the rest of the week off." I hung up and jumped in the car.

"Let's get out of here."

July 19th, Friday.

I went to the dealership and worked at the office. Took one of the cars for a ride and checked for surveillance. Nothing.

July 20th, Saturday.

Family time, but I was too stressed to enjoy it. Happiness and joy as foreign to my life as hope and peace. I decided to go to a ranch in Corona, about an hour drive, to get a little lamb for a ritual. That night I had a nightmare. I was in a jail's bathroom wearing an orange jumpsuit. Two guys were threatening me.

July 21st, Sunday.

I woke-up trembling with a bad premonition. *Should I transfer the load to Tustin? But, what if I go down during the transfer?*

We barbequed and played in the swimming pool. In the evening, after the children went to sleep, I took a shower and dressed on my ceremonial clothing. Then as part of the protection ritual I sacrificed the small lamb to my enslaved spirit. There is power in the blood.

My practices of Palo-Mayombe had increased to almost every day. I consulted and requested my muerto for guidance, protection, and prosperity. I had moved the cauldron and the spiritual tools into a shed outside of the house, an area protected from snooping neighbors by a high wall.

I blew cigar smoke and sprayed a mouth-full of rum into the cauldron as I chanted the spells. I had recorded the Padrino's chants secretly, made a transcript, and memorized them, so I could do the rituals without his help. If he'd known about it, he would blame my mischief on that, of course.

July 22nd, Monday.

I went to the dealership and worked on the car's inventory and paperwork, then, holed up in the second floor offices. I had outfitted one of the upstairs offices as a jewelry studio and worked on an 18 karat gold talisman for protection. The inch-and-a-half-long bow with an arrow encrusted with a big pear-shaped ruby, dark as a drop of blood, supposed to be dedicated to Ochosi, the saint or deity that represents justice and hunters. It didn't keep the law enforcement agencies away though.

July 23rd, Tuesday.

I delivered 200 kilos without incident.

July 24th, Wednesday.

I made an appointment for lunch in a restaurant in Tustin, waited there for a while but the person didn't show up. As I was walking out I saw a tall guy, attitude and all, eating out of a take-out box by the corner of the restaurant. I walked towards him and saw his necklace, a gold map of Colombia with an emerald where Cali was supposed to be.

"What's up?" I nodded once. "Are you Cruces?"

"Ricardo?" He asked.

"Yes." Ricardo was my name for that week. Then, Marcos, Tomas, Samuel, every week a new name for the trade.

He was standing with a foot up on the low wall, in a

nonchalant way, but so out-of-place. *This is too much. This is not your Colombian neighborhood pub, and we were not tourists on an outing either.* His behavior was so obvious that I wanted to hide under a car. I felt like everybody knew we were drug dealers.

"I was waiting for you inside."

"I'm waiting for my driver." He bit on a rib, barbeque sauce running down his chin.

"Let's go." I commanded.

He wiped the sauce with his hand, grabbed his box of ribs and walked beside me. "Where are we going?"

"You will see."

"My driver is not here yet." He slowed down.

I stopped and turned. "I'll show you something, okay?"

"I need to call my driver."

"Don't worry, come on." I waved him to follow.

I had spent the morning checking the area and had left a car behind the shopping center. The restaurant where the meeting took place was in the corner of the strip-mall, and there was a Sushi bar towards the end of the line of shops.

We walked away from the restaurant and as we passed behind the van, I said, "That white van is your load," and handed him the keys.

"But, my driver-"

"Call me to confirm the amount, and keep the van." I said over my shoulder.

I didn't look back, walked towards the shops, into the Sushi bar, straight out the back door, got in my car, and drove away.

July 25th, Thursday.

I made another delivery to a new contact without any trouble. Doubt filled my mind and I felt shaky. *Am I imagining things?*

July 26th, Friday.

I set up the appointment for the next meeting at a restaurant in Laguna Niguel. My plan was to park the loaded truck then call them from a payphone to tell them where it was. No physical contact at all.

I drove a van and parked it by the back of the restaurant where I could see it from the payphone. Got to the payphone and searched my pockets. Nothing. I had forgotten their number at the Auto dealership's office. I only carried my driver's license on deliveries. If I got stopped I had no information about the stash house or clients. I didn't even have my new bug detector because I was driving one of my vans. Now, I had to go inside the restaurant and deliver the keys.

This was one of the new numbers Simon had given me. In a way I was relieved by having to meet the clients. They could have reported no transaction and kept the load.

A cold rush went down my body the moment I walked in the restaurant. They were the same people that had given me the hot van. I sat with them and as we started to talk, a small boy came from a table nearby. It was his son.

Who would bring his son to a meeting? He would have to be totally careless, or totally covered. I gave him the loaded van's keys, and got out of there, fighting the desire to run.

I called Simon. "Spoke with Simon and gave him two hundred dollars for groceries, as you told me" I confirmed the delivery.

"Okay."

"He had car trouble last week. Why did you give me a new number for him?"

"I didn't know it was him. I just get the numbers-"

"That is not cool. You're gonna get me in trouble." I rumbled.

"I'll tell them in the office."

"Sure…bye." I hung up.

Nothing happened, which made me think that my helper was right. Maybe I was just overworked and paranoid. Still, a constant feeling of dread followed me like a hungry dog. I was exhausted, drained. I'd been delivering only once a day and still my planning had gotten sloppy.

My weakened confidence prompted side glances from my helper.

"You are seeing things." she accused.

"No kidding, really." Sarcasm and bitterness dripped. I was shaky and felt like crying. *Was the helicopter last week a product of my imagination? Am I really seeing things? I can't lose it right now. Get a hold of yourself Jack. It's gonna be okay. Maybe she's right. I wish she's right.*

I wanted to stop, I wanted to walk away, but I couldn't. I felt the heat, like a burnt smell on my clothing. I was scared, but I thought I could pull this last one project.

Somehow I managed to have a civilized weekend with my family.

July 29th, Monday.

I planned a delivery to Cruces at the Laguna Hills mall.

I had received a couple loads in white pickup trucks with bed coverings that I didn't have to return. So I passed them to the clients as I finished the projects. No need for a fleet of hot trucks in my shop or parked around the neighborhood.

I arrived at the mall, gave Cruces the keys and told him where the loaded truck was parked, and then walked inside. Again, I left out of the back, and drove off in one of my dealership's cars which I'd left there earlier.

I liked that pickup truck, so I told Cruces to drop it at the same strip mall in Irvine where I had run from the helicopter. Not a good choice, but by now I was starting to believe my wife was right. *Maybe I was seeing things. Nothing has happened...yet.*

Cruces didn't call to let me know the truck was back at the appointed place.

Cruces didn't call at all.

16 THE FALL

July 30th, Tuesday.

Nervous about Cruces, I drove to Newport Beach and had lunch in a restaurant by the marina. It had a small seating area by the payphones. Cruces didn't answer my call within 10 minutes so I drove to Irvine and paged him from inside an office building. Again, waited a few minutes, not wanting to be picked up by the police while waiting for the call –if he had been arrested, the police could trace the number in his pager to the payphone I was calling from- I was about to leave when Cruces answered. He was going to drop the truck later at the place we'd agreed before. "Partied hardy…sorry." Was his excuse.

That evening I told my helper I had to pick up a car for the dealership and she drove me to the area. She dropped me off behind the building where she had picked me up before. The pleasant summer evening breeze unveiled a universe of stars. It was peaceful, in sharp contrast with the roaring of the helicopter the last time I'd been there. I walked towards the truck seating in the middle of the nearly-deserted parking lot. The gas station on my right was closed and dark. Then, two cars drove into the lot from opposite directions. One of the vehicles came from my right and behind, the other from the front left. As I approached the truck, the one in front turned towards me on the next row. Out of the corner of my eye, I saw the headlights of the other one turning into the next parking lane. Now, if I got in the truck I would be boxed between them.

I knelt and pretended to tie my shoelace. They continued slowly on their paths. I stood, walked past the truck, and looked around pretending I was looking for someone. *Who had the tail? Was it mine? Who was the snitch? Was Cruces busted, and now working for the police?* I called my helper from the payphone and she picked me up. They didn't follow.

July 31st, Wednesday.

I felt bad continuing the deliveries knowing that any time the curtain could close and the show would be over, not to mention I could be passing the tail to everyone I had contact with. What else could I do? Besides, somewhere in the back of my mind, somewhere in this crazy carrousel, I thought I'd make it through. It'd happened before.

Maybe I was wrong. Maybe the stress clouded my mind. Maybe, I was going to finish without problems. Maybe it was time to retire.

After a restless sleep, I got up, took a cold shower, and got dressed. Tania and I made plans to have sushi for lunch at a restaurant in Laguna Niguel, and I went down to the kitchen to have breakfast. My son, seated on the highchair, splashed oatmeal as the babysitter fed him, and my stepdaughter ate her cereal at the kitchen table.

"Why are you wearing shorts, Dad? Aren't you going to the

office?" She held a spoonful in mid air.

"No tie today. I have a short day at work, pumpkin."

I didn't know how short the day was going to be, or how long, depending of the perspective. I gave her a kiss on the forehead.

"I love you, Daddy."

"I love you too, pumpkin." My heart ached every time she said she loved me. I didn't deserve it.

I walked to my son's highchair and ruffled his hair. He reached and grabbed my finger. I kissed the top of his head. "I love you, son."

He giggled. Looking at me, he mimicked. "Wowu onnn."

"Bye Martha, have a good day." I smiled at the babysitter, and kissed my son again.

"Bye, Señor."

I drove around making phone calls to arrange a delivery. We agreed to meet at a restaurant in Laguna Niguel, not too far from were I was going to have lunch with my wife. That way, I could drop the loaded car, and walk to lunch, finishing another day of work with a good meal.

When I turned in to the garage of the stash house, I noticed a parked light blue pickup truck, with tinted windows and a high camper-shell, parked on the line of sight.

Memory of the dream, the jail vision, and the desire to transfer of the load, became a churning block of ice in my stomach.

Inside the garage, I loaded the ten cardboard boxes with

twenty kilos each. Only one hundred and seventy kilos to go and the project would be finished.

Back in the truck, I turned on the engine and pushed the garage door opener. Moaning and cracking the garage door slowly opened, and I backed out. The truck appeared in the rearview mirror, and I imagined the detectives inside reporting, "Suspect driving out now."

I drove out of the complex and took Moulton Parkway. I liked delivering during the late morning hours because the streets were fairly clear.

Continuing on Moulton Parkway, I checked my mirrors and took mental note of the cars around me. At the corner of La Paz Road I got in the turning lane and waited for the light to change. There was a Camaro two cars behind. I had bad experiences with Camaros before, the same tone of blue, but a newer model now. Fast and macho, the undercover ride special.

At the corner of Paseo de Valencia I could go right and to Cabot Road, and if any car continued on La Paz then made the right turn at Cabot, it would confirm the tail. At Cabot Road, I made a right and so did the blue Camaro. He got behind me.

At Crown Valley Parkway I waited for some traffic to pass and made a right turn. Up the hill on Crown Valley Parkway, he followed. When I got to the intersection of Greenfield Drive there was a police cruiser there, in the turning lane coming the opposite way. We were going to be on the same road soon.

I made the right turn. The cruiser, lights flashing, jumped the red light.

Looking at the patrol's lights in the rearview mirror, it all seemed unreal. Like an out-of-the-body experience. I passed the restaurant where the delivery was supposed to happen, then the Sushi place on my left. *What was Tania going to think when I don't show up for lunch? If I call her now, she would be implicated. Could I still get out of this one?*

Then the helicopter circled and descended as I continued driving towards Nellie Gail Ranch with a growing tail of patrols and unmarked police cars.

My past flashed through my mind. I remembered the people, the misery, and the pain. I imagined Satan laughing as my life swirled towards the drain.

All I'd done for money and dreams, dreams of a better life, a family, a home. The reality of it all, my dreams had been stolen by my own greed. Money hadn't brought me any happiness and joy. I had thrown money to the people around me and they all had smiled and danced to my tune, but the truth was that money couldn't buy love and happiness. Diamond smiles turned into grins of shattered glass.

Money didn't fill the hole in my heart, no matter how much, there was always more wanting. Now, a little too late, I realized that no money was worth missing my son's childhood or all my mom's suffering.

Again, I looked at the red and blue lights on the rear view mirror wishing them to disappear. Wishing it was all a bad dream. My wife was going to be furious. I wondered what was going to happen to them. *We'll have to postpone our lunch honey.* My beautiful ballerina, she could dance like a hummingbird, and roar like a lion. She had a temper. I will always love her.

As I continued driving the undercover police cars lined up behind the patrol as the officer yelled through his car's PA, "Pull over now!"

This was the end of my criminal career, and I doubted I'd

walk the streets again. These were my last moments of freedom.

"Pull over and stop now." Woop-woop, woop-woop. The siren sounded far away. Like a dimmed TV set.

The helicopter circled in of front my windshield like a crazy bee, like a huge beetle. It was my favorite kind of helicopter, a Hughes 500, fast and quiet, gold with a stripe, such a gorgeous machine. I never got to fly one of those….

Trapped by my own desires, captive by my own preferences, enticed and deceived by my greedy heart, I had come to the end of the road.

I pulled over and they swarmed like mad flies.

The policeman approached and told me to step out, didn't even tell me why he was stopping me. Well, there were no tinted windows this time…

I obeyed, and he told me to sit by the curb, between the cruiser and the truck.

The agent in charge asked, "May we search your truck?"

"No."

"Why not?"

"There are two answers to your question, 'Yes or No.' I choose 'No'."

"We're going to search anyway." He waved a detective to go ahead.

A stocky Latino unlocked the bed cover of the pick up, climbed inside, and opened one box. He waved a kilo with a shout of victory, joined by the other officers. He sliced the wrapping, and put a knife-tip full of white scales in a testing vial, shaking it, the liquid inside turned blue, bringing more yelping and high-five's.

The oversized policeman guarding me pointed a fat finger at me. "Don't get any ideas."

I looked at his bulk and smiled. *One thing I'm sure of is that you won't be the one catching me.* "Right." I stared at the pavement.

The agent in charge turned from the action to me. "Stand up and turn around."

He cuffed my hands behind, led me to a cruiser, and I got in. One of the detectives passed by and waved good bye. His mocking smile branded in my brain.

I looked at him. "I am gone…and a thousand will come." As I had replaced someone in the chain, replacements for me were already in place, business as usual.

The evil machine didn't stop. It continued eating and destroying lives. I felt powerless against my own evil desires, another pawn in my master's game. The enemy within had won.

A blond detective opened the door of the cruiser and told me to step out. He took my elbow and led me to the blue Camaro. After removing one handcuff, he had me put my hands in front, and cuffed them again. He opened the passenger's door and I got in. After giving some instructions to another detective he climbed on the driver's seat and we took off.

We chatted as he drove north on the Interstate 5. Except for the cuffs, I felt like a hitch-hiker going for a ride, a long ride. Traffic was light. After a while, he exited the freeway and stopped at a red light.

I looked at the sidewalk. *Could I make it if I run now? They would make my family's life impossible. Besides, I'd have to…get clothing, money, head to Mexico, and then down to Colombia. What would they do to my wife…did they get her?*

Out of the corner of my eye I could see the detective looking forward. *Would he shoot me?*

We got to the Anaheim Police Department's back parking lot and he got out, then opened my door. I followed while he took off his ankle holster and gun and put it inside the trunk. Right there, I could bend over and get it. He put his service pistol inside the trunk also. I looked at the gun and back at him and smiled. He smiled back. "Let's go."

He led me through the station and as I walked in the booking area, I saw my wife crying and trembling inside a small holding cell.

My heart ached. "Hey hon, how are you doing?"

"I went looking for you at the condo and was banging on the garage door when they got me." Terror filled her big eyes and mascara ran down her cheeks.

"What did you tell them?"

"They took me to a field and questioned me."

My stomach turned. "A field? Where? What do you mean?"

"Behind a housing tract, I don't know." She shuddered. "After a while they brought me here."

My teeth clenched. "Did they do anything?"

"No, just asked questions and waited…and waited, I was so scared." Her voice trembled. "…then brought me here and a female officer did a body search…so humiliating." She sobbed.

"It'll soon be over." My voice lacked conviction but she didn't seem to notice.

Her eyes widened. "What is going to happen now?"

I lowered my voice to a whisper. "I am going away for a long time. Hopefully they'll let you go. Let me see what I can do."

The detective turned me over to the booking officer then left. A deputy took my fingerprints and showed me to an interrogation room. After a long wait in the tiny room, the Latino that had searched the truck and the blond that had driven me entered.

The Latino started. "How are you doing?"

I shrugged. "Fine." I looked up from the desk. "What's going to happen to my wife?"

"Who do you work with?" He leaned on the table.

"I work alone." I looked back to the top of the desk.

"All that cocaine…by yourself? No helpers?" The blond detective sat.

"No workers, nobody to kill, or to kill me."

I guessed they were waiting for other people to show up at the stash house while they questioned me.

"We'll let your wife go if you agree to let us search the family's home and the business. The Latino offered.

Relief washed over me. There was only a small amount of

cash in a hidden safe at the home office. "Sure. Go ahead."

They went out and afterwards, the Latino detective took me to a small holding cell with a phone on the wall. I figured they were going to record all conversations but, so what? There was nothing to hide anymore.

When I called my wife, she was relieved to be back with the children, and asked for the combination to my office's safe. I gave her the numbers, and calmed her down. Officers were going through everything, and she worried about the neighbors seeing all the police cars in front of the house, but that was the least of my problems. At least she was free to take care of the children, arrange for an attorney, and communicate with Simon.

The home search embarrassed my mother-in-law – smile –.

The officers spread out to the yard and discovered the *Palo Mayombe* cauldrons. My wife told me the Latino detective had stumbled back, spooked. "I'm not going near *that*." They took pictures and left the artifacts alone.

The auto dealership's cars were confiscated but the jewelry equipment was left alone.

At the jail, it was time to get settled for the night. The Latino detective came to visit later and asked if I needed something.

"A jet to Jamaica and a million dollars would do." I smiled. "How about a book?"

"Let me see what I can find." He came back later and gave me an action novel about Vietnam's war.

Reading became a habit to cherish.

A few days latter I was taken to the court building in Santa

Ana and charged. It sounded funny pleading innocent, kind of stupid, but I did it anyway.

Bail was set at forty million dollars. I laughed, who did they think I was, Pablo Escobar?

The District Attorney said that the street value of the load was worth two hundred and fifty million dollars, and that was the value the Judge took into consideration for the initial bail. I wished I had clients that paid the D.A.s prices.

A few weeks later my attorney filed a motion for a bail reduction and it was lowered to twenty-five million. I settled in for the long haul and hoped to beat the case on a technicality.

The three charges-the Cruces' load, the load I was driving with, and the rest they found at the stash house-totaling over five hundred kilos could carry a sentence of over fifty-four years if found guilty by trial.

PART TWO

CHRIST

17 GET ME OUT OF HERE!

I was taken to the booking area, and for the first time in my life saw God's love in action. As Deputy Lyons took my fingerprints, he said that God loved me, and quoted Isaiah chapter 55:6-7.

> Seek the Lord while He may be found,
>
> Call upon Him while He is near.
>
> Let the wicked forsake his way,
>
> And the unrighteous man his thoughts;
>
> Let him return to the Lord,
>
> And He will have mercy on him;
>
> And to our God,
>
> For He will abundantly pardon.

I listened.

He continued sharing, Jeremiah 29:11-13.

For I know the thoughts that I think toward you, says the Lord,

Thoughts of peace and not of evil, to give you a future and a hope.

Then you will call upon Me and go and pray to Me,

And I will listen to you.

And you will seek Me and find Me,

When you search for Me with all your heart.

He looked so peaceful. There was something different about him. I expected a policeman, a law abiding citizen, to be disgusted by me. I expected hatred to pour out from this man used to handling the trash of the world, the waste of society, but no.

Deputy Lyons smiled and shared. He honestly cared.

I deserved punishment for my crimes, but there he was, treating me better than most people treat each other. Was that weird? Yes! *It was weird!* Someone who actually cared for a total stranger was out of the ordinary. It was weird in the most wonderful way, a not-of-this-world experience.

What I had sown, I was now reaping. Regardless of the factors behind my actions, I had ignored the rules and rebelled against authority. Now I had to pay. Those Scriptures helped me to recognize my faults, and gave me hope. They gave me a glimpse of what the future held if I sought God. I was to bank on those scriptures in years to come.

In my quest through New Age, Wicca, White and Black Magic, Satanism, Santeria and Palo Mayombe, I'd never found peace, or an answer to the emptiness in my life. I practiced divination through Tarot cards, runes and *cocos* - round pieces of coconut shell used in Santeria - but usually interpreted the readings for my own benefit.

The bottom line was that between my beliefs and Deputy Lyons', both of us could be wrong, but both of us couldn't be right. Either one was right and the other wrong, or we were both wrong. I had been reaching out to gods, and now, I found God reaching out to *me* through this man. It made more sense. This God was not a god of my own creation. I didn't want a god made at my image, or with my understanding of power. A small god could not help me. I needed the Creator of the Universe, a God omnipresent –be present everywhere-, omnipotent –all powerful-, and omniscient –all knowing. I needed a God who would be with me forever and everywhere, a God who could do beyond what I needed or asked, and a God that knew what was best for me. That was the God I needed.

My Catholic upbringing had given me a basic understanding of God, but I lacked the scriptural foundation to apply to my life. I had no idea about God's promises, requirements, of what He expected of me.

My ways had gotten me nowhere.

The scriptures Deputy Lyons gave me pointed the way at the right time. He planted a seed of hope.

After the booking process, I waited for the transfer to the Orange County Jail. There were at least one hundred men in the stinky cell. Everyone talked over the voices of the others. I sat along the wall on the concrete bench minding my own business. Sweaty and sticky, without a shower in three days, I was more than cranky.

One young Latino with a shaved head approached me. "Give me your shoes." He pointed to my leather sandals.

I looked up, and then looked down at my sandals. *Was he going to walk in jail with my leather sandals?* -I cursed- "I am not in the mood for this. Go play with your friends over there, okay?" I waved him away.

He looked puzzled, as if not expecting the lamb to roar, then turned around and went back to his group of gangsters.

I walked to the open bathroom with filthy walls covered with graffiti and trash all around, it smelled awful. Used toilet paper littered a corner. A prisoner stood behind me. "What did you do to get a 40 million bail?"

I glimpsed over my shoulder. He looked like a college student, wide-rimmed eye glasses, greasy black hair, pale, and skinny. "I don't know what they are talking about."

Others were more discrete, some wanted connections, others information, all of a sudden I had a full spectrum of partners and soldiers. Either way, I had enough problems already. I couldn't believe people in jail wanted to keep dealing. Besides, to me everyone was an outsider and a potential informant, so I played my part. No need to remind people of their stupidity, after all, we were all in the same boat. An outcast outside, an outcast inside, I didn't need friends before, and I didn't want them now.

At the Orange County Jail, I was put in the "fish tank" with all the catch of the day. Sitting in a corner, I heard a familiar voice rambling. "It's not right that they arrested me, I am innocent. I am just a driver…Don't know anything."

I stood up to take a better look, and through the crowd I saw Cruces's driver. His tangled white hair and beard told me he'd been in custody probably as long as I had. He could pass for a wino, but I knew he was sharp, maybe too sharp. *Was he the informant?* This was not good, definitely not good. My hope was that they had no witnesses, and with a good attorney, I would be able to beat the case through a technicality.

I approached him from behind and whispered in his ear, "Shut up, you're only making it worse." He turned. His pale blue eyes sparkled as my nose almost touched his. "Shut up." I hissed as I looked into his eyes, turned and walked away never to see him again. I had met him briefly at a transfer.

My mistake, now he'd remember me for sure.

The next familiar face I saw was Cruces. About a week later, at the next court appearance as I looked at the cell across the aisle where the prisoners in protective custody were, the *blue banders* – they had a blue ID wristband. "PCs," snitches, child molesters, and other prisoners segregated from the general population. He slouched.

I was shocked and angry. Not only the thought of him testifying against me, but knowing what would happen to him if he did. I would have no control over it. He would be killed. "Hey, what are you doing, are you crazy? You know what is gonna happen."

"Hey, you can't talk to them. Why are you talking to a snitch?" A tattooed youngster, on the bench across from me, stood and approached me.

"He is going to testify against me, okay? Mind your own business." I growled at the stocky Latino.

"They can add another charge for that." Another volunteered.

"Really? No kidding. Like I care." I smirked and wiggled my head.

How much worse could it get? I looked at the cell across the hallway. *I may as well kill him.* Cruces stared at the floor.

Hours later, at the court's session, when it was time for Cruces to speak, I couldn't help it and yelled, "Don't do it, man." But he pleaded guilty anyway. What I didn't know was –my attorney told me later- that he'd agreed to testify against the people in his organization also.

When it was my turn, my attorney stood. "Your Honor, he is only a mule..." His words agreed with the District Attorney's statement, and they felt like the last nail in my coffin. I fired him.

The legal system, like a negotiation process, required a heavy presence at the table. I hired a high profile attorney and he gave me confidence. Nevertheless the court appearances became just postponements and time passed with no real progress. In a way that helped to decrease attention on the case, after a few months I was just another prisoner.

In between, Simon sent a message to Tania; I had to pay a million dollars for the load. I reported how the arrest had happened, and that the fault came from whoever had passed the hot numbers for the deliveries. Now, he had to pay my fee for the load *and* the attorney's expenses. He was responsible.

He didn't agree, so through an acquaintance, I found someone to handle the collection. For a percentage, an immediate payment was *negotiated*.

Upset about my procedures, Simon expressed his feelings, "I am going to kill you when you get out Mono."

What a stupid thing to say. It would be easier to get me

killed inside.

Months dragged on, and my hope dimmed.

I sought spiritual guidance through Santeria practices inside the cell even though it provided no peace or solutions.

My attorney came one evening. "The San Diego District Attorney took Cruces in custody, and now he wants to talk to you." He looked worried. "The DEA had Cruces under surveillance, but lost him, until they found out he was here…in your case."

"What do you mean? Why the DEA didn't arrests us in the first place? Why did they let Anaheim Police Department take the case?"

"I don't know, Jack."

Is this going to become a federal case now? What's going on? Are the Feds going to pick me up also?" The room spun.

"I don't know…We just have to wait and see."

"When…When do we know?" I leaned on the table, deflated.

"Anytime. The D.A. didn't tell me." He got up.

"I'll see you." I shook his hand.

"Good night, Jack. Call me if he comes."

"Sure. Good night, thanks for coming." I went back to my cell.

Now I was scared, the Federal system gave longer sentences and their conviction rate was much higher. It meant life in prison for sure.

I prayed, "God, get me out of this one and I will follow you for the rest of my life."

Uncertainty tortured me day and night. A couple of weeks later, the San Diego District Attorney came, and with him a DEA agent as big as a refrigerator, his suit jacket could cover a small car.

"Hey man, you know steroids are bad for you, right?" I joked.

He smiled.

After the introductions, the D.A. showed me some pictures, and in the middle of the spread was Cruces' driver. "You know I know him." I said pointing at his picture. "You can expect me to tell the truth, as much as I expect it from you." I stared at him. "I know him, but I don't know anybody else." I tapped the picture, trying to ease the uncomfortable silence. The black and white 8x10s seemed like 1960's mug shots. "They all look the same." I wiped my sweaty hands on the pants of the jumpsuit.

"Who is your connection in Colombia?"

"Alvaro." I stared at him.

"What's his last name?"

"We don't use last names in the business. I'm not even sure that is his real name. The less I know, the longer I live. That's my motto."

"So you don't know anybody else in those pictures?" He pointed to the guys on the left.

They looked familiar, but, the truth was, I didn't know the names of most of the people.

"Is my case going to become Federal?"

He gave me a blank stare, like he didn't understand my English. I wanted to jump over the table and shake the answer out of him. The gorilla smiled.

"We'll see. I'll let your attorney know." He got up, and the monkey followed. "Good bye Mr. Rausch." He walked out. The gorilla turned and gave me a mischievous smile.

People talked about carpeted dayrooms and upholstered chairs. "The Federal system is so much better…" I couldn't understand why a carpet or softer chair appealed to these guys. Prison is prison. Especially if the sentence could double, it consumed me, waiting for the curtain to fall. My only card was that the Feds would have to give my attorney access to the informant. The Confrontation Clause of the Sixth Amendment to the Constitution gave my attorney the opportunity to cross-examine all the witnesses, including the informant. In high-profile cases, sometimes they let the smaller fish walk –in this case I hoped it was me- to protect the infiltrated individual.

At the same time the State proceedings continued without interruption.

Those first months in jail were horrible, the smells, the crowds, the food, and the cold cells. Some Correctional Officers were nice, and some were very nasty. The nice ones were Christians. The nasty ones seemed contaminated by the evil they had to deal with day in and day out. I felt their frustration, anger, and hatred. It scared me to be at their will. There were horror stories about rebels taken into rooms by a group of officers and coming out badly injured. But who could believe anyone here? This was lawsuit-happy California. Inmates filed lawsuits for broken cookies. Nevertheless, my rebelliousness dimmed with time, and I learned respect for authority. Adapting is the key to survival. Some things changed, others stayed the same. The building's smell of disinfectant, the rumble of the Air Conditioners, the constant pulsating hum, and the echoing voices and screams, made me feel I was on a cruise to Hell.

I had been placed in a hundred-man dorm divided by race, Whites, Blacks, Chicanos (Mexican-Americans), Mexicans, and Others. Usually the classification process assigned Colombians to the Mexican group, or to the "Others" group; Asians, Mid-Easterners, Filipinos, etc.

When I came in the dorm, the shot-callers, or leaders, asked me which race I was and what group I wanted to "run with" or belong to. I decided to run with the Chicanos because they were more dangerous, and I got an instant troop of soldiers. It worked well for a while, until one of our crew took the tennis shoes of a White, and sparked a riot. I couldn't understand that behavior. It's a matter of power, but still, it seemed ridiculous to fight for State property. In those riots, people got hurt, even died, and some guys picked up new charges, even life in prison.

As a result of the melee, the Deputies entered the dorm and threw everything on the floor -a shake down- the pillows, the mattresses, the canteen, everything, and stepped on it. I didn't know what compiled more madness, the riot, or the officers' behavior. One for one, but nothing made sense. After that, most of the Chicanos' crew got transferred, and the ones left were on edge.

So I spoke with the Mexican shot-caller and told him I wanted to run with them. He didn't care. They just minded their business and did their time peacefully. At lunch time, as I got in line to go to the mess hall, the Chicano behind me said, "Hey, only the shot-caller walks in front."

I turned. "I am not on the front of the Chicanos. I am the last of the Mejicanos."

"Why are you running with them now?" He growled.

"You guys are out of control. I don't need more trouble." I turned and continued walking.

The single line moved out of the dorm, and before turning into the main corridor, when we were out of sight of the dorm's officer, he pushed me. "You have to go to the back."

I turned, and he swung. I avoided the punch, but his momentum carried him. I grabbed him in a choke hold, pushed him to the floor, and hit him on the face with the right fist.

The building's alarm screamed and the deputy on the walkway came running. "Get down, get down." He screamed at the inmates. He turned the corner, pulled his pepper-spray canister, and hit me with a burst on the forehead.

I didn't feel anything, so I got up and walked to pick-up my eyeglasses fallen a few feet away.

"Get on the floor, on the floor now." The officer yelled.

The building's alarm added to my confusion.

Other officers came running. "On the floor now. Everyone, get on the floor."

I was in a haze. "He attacked me." I pointed to the guy on the floor, as I straightened a bend in my glasses, put them on, and then sat.

After reporting the incident as under control, and the line of inmates gone to the dining hall, the officer took me to the infirmary area on another floor. He told me to get into an empty room, walls covered with dark brown rubber, and only a hole on the floor by the corner. It looked like a room for mental patients in horror movies.

"Didn't the pepper spray burn?" He pointed to the corner. "Get in there."

"A little, not that bad…"

"Get undressed…have to wash it off."

I walked inside the somber room and undressed. *I hope they don't leave me in here.*

Another officer hosed me down, and then gave me a towel along with another set of clothing. Afterwards, I was taken downstairs to the booking area. The first punishment for any altercation was a transfer that required going through classification all over again. It took the whole day. Depending on the severity of the case, classification could also effect housing, and privileges, like the frequency of visits and the right to have commissary.

The system started with a white ID band, then after a few write-ups, yellow band, and the final red band, for high power – known gang leaders- or most dangerous inmates. Most wore it with pride. Like ranks in the military.

Hours later, I was assigned to the IRC, Intake and Release Center, a maximum security area, consisting of tanks with two tiers of two-men cells with the officers' tower in the middle.

After a couple of weeks, I had a hearing with the IRC's Sergeant and was sentenced to ten days in the "Hole"-solitary confinement-where I spent my first Thanksgiving Day of my life as a prisoner.

Time goes really slow in the Hole. I was under suicide

watch, a standard procedure. It was freezing, and I spent most of the time wrapped in the blanket with only my nose out.

A previous guest had drawn a life size woman on the wall, and she kept me company. It was a nice drawing. She looked like my first wife. Every hour, the officer called out my last name through the screen on the door, and I was required to wave a hand or look out from my cocoon, and recite my booking number. I only got up to eat, and workout, two hundred push-ups and two hundred squats. The exercise helped me sleep. Showers were every other day. There was a cardboard box by the showers with books, and my reading habit continued to grow.

After the ten days, I was sent to the IRC again. It was more peaceful because I only had to deal with one other inmate. The cell had a metal table and two stools attached to the wall, the stainless steel toilet and sink unit at the back, and the bunk beds on the side. It was cramped up but still better than the dorm. The bottom bed was concrete with an opening under it to put our supplies and groceries. Once a week, with money put on my account, I was able to get a variety of supplies. My bed, the top one, was metal bolted to the wall. The front of the cell and door consisted of a metal frame with thick glass. Only one of the two ceiling lights could be turned off. The mattress covered in thick plastic, was one inch thick, if you were lucky to have a newer one.

I quickly learned the trade system. When someone came with a better mattress, and had a short sentence, a chocolate bar would reserve it. Before his transfer and at a time of dayroom and shower, the mattress trade had to be done quickly so the officers wouldn't interfere. Candy purchased at the canteen also bought new clothing and shoes. The trade was made inside the cleaning buckets in plastic bags. The trustees –volunteer prisoners- would pick up their candy, and the next day, I would have my new underwear or even a new jumpsuit. To keep my new clothing, I washed it by hand and hanged it to dry on the vent. Otherwise, I had to exchange it weekly, and get whatever they gave me, usually worn out and torn replacements. Washing my clothing with hand soap bought at the canteen, made it smell good and kept it in good condition. Especially to go to court, I wanted to look, or at least smell clean. Little things like that lifted my spirit.

We had two hours a day in the *dayroom* for shower, TV, and to make collect calls. I didn't miss the one-hundred-man dorm, or gladiator school as it was called. I adjusted well to the system. The key was not to get transferred.

What amazed me the most was that everyone wanted to deal, connections abounded.

18 THE MAKER

The Christmas blues hit me pretty hard. Sheets of rain played with the lights decorating the buildings across the street as I watched through the narrow windows of my cell. My wife visited less. If lucky, I saw the kids once a month.

My cellmate, "Q", an African-American, clean, quiet, and respectful, made the program easier. Incarceration didn't get any better than that. He read the Bible and minded his own business. He was about my height, in his early twenties, fit, and with a good attitude. He had perfect teeth and his smile lit the whole room.

One night, he came back from church singing and smiling. I asked him, "What's up with you? You're facing life in prison, and here you are, all happy as if you were getting out tonight."

He beamed. "It doesn't matter what they accuse me of. My Lord Jesus paid for all my sins."

"You' crazy, bro. You' goin' down." I needled, but curiosity moved me.

"I know I am a sinner. God sent Jesus Christ to die for my sins so I could be forgiven and be in peace with Him. It's all here."

He tapped his Bible.

Nobody had explained the Gospel to me that way. I hardly passed the Catechism class.

Q invited me to the next church service.

Next week, when the officer announced it through the PA, we stood by the cell's glass door signaling eagerly. At the service, we sang a few songs; the Pastor read a passage from the Bible and explained it.

It was December 15, 1996. I had spent over four months inside seeing the effect of drugs on the prisoners' lives, and thinking about the devastation in their families and mine afflicted me. The guilt overwhelmed me. The message not only convicted me but it also provided a solution. The Pastor explained that God's pure nature and justice required a payment for my faults. That was a high call. How could I ever repay, how could I ever restore the damages done by my actions? I calculated that approximately 40 million people–including addicts and family members-had been affected by the cocaine I'd distributed. How could I fix *that*?

The damage was irreversible.

The Pastor said that before God, I was forgiven if I *repented* of my faults and *believed* that Jesus' sacrifice paid my debt in full. God had sent Him to die for my sin and by His death and resurrection I could have eternal life. All I had to do was to believe. (Romans 1:2-5; 3:23; 5:8; 6:23; John 3:16-18;17:3; 20:31; Ephesians 2:8-9; Acts 26:23).

I gave my life to God.

I prayed, "Father God, I repent from all my sins. Jesus Christ, thanks for Your sacrifice for me, I accept You as my personal Savior, fill me with Your Holy Spirit and guide me through Your Word. In Jesus' name I pray. Amen."

I called all my family and told them about Jesus but they dismissed it as something they already knew about.

Nobody was going to do my time, but knowing that I had peace with God lifted a weight off my shoulders. I had no problem understanding that I was a sinner; the bright orange jumpsuit gave me a loud and clear message about it. Now, changing my way of thinking, reacting, and trusting God for the solutions, became a real challenge.

The pain and suffering my actions had caused to my family, my mom, and my sisters could never be erased, but now I had something positive to share with them and the world.

Set Free Prison Ministries had comprehensive correspondence courses from organizations such as Moody Bible Institute and Emmaus Bible College, which increased my knowledge of God, causing my faith to grow (Romans 10:17).

Doing a study in the morning and another in the afternoon made time fly and occupied my mind with constructive and encouraging concepts.

> Ephesians 1:13 In Him you also trusted, after you heard the word of truth, the gospel of your salvation; in whom also, having believed, you were sealed with the Holy Spirit of promise.

Now the Holy Spirit helped me to understand that the feelings of guilt were also a call from God to come to Him. When I analyzed what Jesus told his disciples in John 14:15-17, I realized that His Spirit had been around convicting me, calling me for that day when I received His forgiveness, and now His Spirit lived in me, teaching, correcting, and guiding me (John 14:26; 15:26-27;

16:7-15; Acts 1:8).

Jesus said it, I believed it, and I wanted it. It was all in the Bible.

I knew enough about the spiritual world to recognize the difference about Satan's influence and lies versus this wonderful presence within me. The Holy Spirit renewed me. By reading the Bible, and learning about his promises, I knew I could trust Him.

God always comes through for His people.

I wanted to let all the anger and bitterness go, but I had to face the pain and the truth. The enemy within, covered in layers of denial and frustration, years of ignoring the real issues and rationalizing my actions, made him a stealthier target than I'd expected.

One thing I wasn't prepared for was to fight spiritually. Satan, my destructive ally, became my daily enemy along with his demons. Worst of all, his seeds of rage, bitterness, abandonment, and fear, all those issues and people I needed to forgive, became my constant adversaries. Like the Trojan Horse's soldiers, these memories came at me from every angle and usually at my weakest times. Nevertheless, as I reached out to help others and share about my faith, my own issues seemed to dissipate and gave me a path to overcome my demons.

I peeled away the layers of deception and brought to God my hardened heart, my pain, my life, my brokenness, the abuse, the rape, the memories that haunted me through the nights, and especially the fear of the future. I needed a heart transplant and God gave it to me. He changed my hardened heart, my emotional brokenness, for a new way of thinking (Ezekiel 36:25-27).

With a new mindset, new motivations and feelings, many

things changed. Now the Jack I knew was fading away. My old identity was gone, I wasn't a criminal or a player anymore, or at least I had a strong desire not to continue in that path. Now I found myself in uncharted territory. What was I going to do for living? Who was I?

Yes, the scriptures said that God will give me a future and a hope, but, how did that work? The Bible gave me peace and hope but I still had to pay my bills, have relationships, survive, how was this going to happen?

It was refreshing to read the Bible and find stories to apply to my life. Like the Valley of the Dry Bones in Ezekiel 37. My life was broken and dry, and God restored it. It was a painful process, but worth it. Experiencing God in my life, and in my way of thinking, was awesome. Facing my daily challenges was another thing.

One morning, I woke up feeling feverish. Sitting on the floor, I hugged the toilet as dry heaves added to the general aches. Cold sweat ran down my trembling body.

I pushed the button for the intercom. "Excuse me, Deputy." No response. *I know you are looking at me from behind the tinted window making wise cracks.*

I pushed the button twice–a big no, no–"Excuse me, Officer. I have high fever and abdominal pain."

A minute later. "Are you bleeding?"

"No, Sir, but I need to see the doctor, my stomach hurts. I have fever and have been throwing up."

"Is it life threatening? Are you bleeding?" Sarcasm dripped out of the aluminum intercom plate.

"Sir, I need to see the doctor, please."

"Who is this?"

"Rausch."

"This is your lucky day. The nurse will be here after breakfast, fill a medical slip and give it to me at chow time."

"Thank you, Sir. I really appreciate it." I sat down and rested my head on my forearms on top of the table.

"Are you going to die on me?" Q joked, "Wait until after you give me your breakfast."

I groaned.

Breakfast came and I gave the medical slip to the deputy. Q enjoyed an extra plate as I lay down waiting for the nurse.

The door buzzed open and the intercom blasted. "Rausch to the nurse station."

Four inmates lined up near the nurses' office. I leaned on the wall and read my bible while waiting my turn.

"Rausch." The nurse called.

I went in, and sat where he told me.

"What is going on?" He scribbled on my chart.

"My stomach hurts." I rubbed my left side.

He reached towards my mouth with a thermometer. "Under the tongue."

He inserted the thermometer and looked at his watch. Then, after reading the temperature, the looked at me with wide eyes, "How long have you had the abdominal   pain?"

"It woke me up. I tried to throw up but only bile came out."

Sweat beaded his forehead as he told me to stand. "Where does it hurt?"

"Here." I touched the left lower abdominal area.

"Sit back down. I think your appendix burst." He picked up the phone. "Need transport to the hospital, possible appendix burst…Yes."

He led me to a holding cell downstairs, then returned a few minutes later and took me outside. The ambulance had the doors open, and a gurney rested by the sidewalk of the fenced transport area.

The blond driver smacked gum and played with her hair. "He doesn't have a busted appendix. He would be screaming."

The nurse pulled his brows together and nearly roared. "Your job is not to diagnose, it's to drive him to the hospital." He held my arm and helped me onto the stretcher.

He turned back at the driver and gave her a scolding. "I am going to write you up. You are not to contradict my diagnosis, just drive him."

I looked at the heavy-set blonde, hoping she didn't take my Bible away or dump me down the road. She waved to the other EMT. They pushed the gurney into the ambulance and closed the doors.

After passing the security gates, we drove away into the morning traffic. No siren, no apparent rush.

I had no idea which hospital they were transferring me to.

At the hospital, a Deputy searched me. Then a female nurse performed a more through search. Between the humiliation and the pain, I felt like dropping dead right there.

Finally the doctor arrived. "Where does it hurt?" He said without a greeting.

"Here." I pointed, and he pushed his finger in the spot.

"Aghhh. Yes, *there!*" I groaned under the painful pressure.

"Prepare him for surgery." He walked away.

His calculating demeanor made me nervous. *Would he sell my liver?* I shuddered. *What else could he take out?*

The nurses prepped me, injected me, and put me on a table with the arms out. I felt crucified…then, nothing.

I woke up groggy and nauseous. The nurse responded to my call and gave me some crushed ice, and then I fell back asleep.

Later, I tried to read my Bible but couldn't concentrate, so I chose a good verse and meditated on it until I drifted off again.

Pain woke me and I called the nurse.

"What's the matter?" She grabbed the chart from the front of the bed.

"I'm not feeling well. I got cramps on my legs, my body aches, and I feel hot."

She turned and left. "I'll be right back," she said over her shoulder.

After a while, she returned. "Are you an organ donor?" She scribbled something on my chart.

"No." I clutched my Bible on my chest, and prayed.

No extra body parts missing, I survived that night.

The appendix had burst, and after the operation the doctor had left a portion of the incision open with a catheter to drain the fluids. I was kept at the hospital for observation. High fever and pain came and went. The days passed with me heavily sedated.

A few days later, Tania came to visit with the kids. I was surprised when the nurse announced I had visitors.

I walked slowly, pushing and supporting myself on the rolling IV tower, following the Deputy in charge of the prisoner's area of the hospital. He opened the door of the visiting room. "Go ahead, take your time." He locked the door behind me.

I leaned forward to ease the pain and walked into the room which was also used for storage. There were boxes, a broken hospital bed, and a chair. The big window to my right revealed the horrified faces of my family. I gave them my best smile.

My wife started to cry and the kids clung to her legs. I grabbed the phone on the wall and she reached for hers. "Do I look that bad?" My heart ached seeing them suffer.

She nodded. "How are you?" Her voice trembled as she spoke between sobs.

"I thought I was gonna die the other night. They asked me if I was an organ donor." I laughed but the pain made me wince. I slumped on the chair. *Lord give me wisdom and strength to say something encouraging.* "It looks like I am going to make it though." I smiled. *At least I could have left the life insurance money.* "How did you find me?"

"We went to visit and they told me you had been transferred here." She sighed. "Say hi to Junior…" She put the phone on my son's ear and he reached out to hold it with both hands.

"Hi son, how are you doing? Are you being a good boy?"

He nodded and looked at mom. At two years old, he probably wondered why I didn't come out and hug him, why I didn't come home…The damage to this innocent boy's life, undoable and immeasurable. "I love you, Junior. I miss you very much. Give the phone to your sister. I pointed to her. He nodded. His huge brown eyes full of questions. My heart ripped.

"Hi daddy, what happened to you?" Christy said with a shy smile.

"I had an operation, Pumpkin. My appendix burst." I fought the knot on my throat and tried not to cry.

"What is the appendix?" The usual shine on her beautiful brown eyes was replaced by a cloud of fear.

Good question, I didn't even know. "A part of the body that, when it gives trouble, the doctor takes it out and everything gets back to normal." *Sounds good to me.* "I am going to be fine, Pumpkin. Don't worry, okay?" I said it with as much conviction as I could muster. "I love you very much. Now, give the phone to mom. Love you…"

"I love you too, Daddy." She put her little hand against the glass.

My hand on the other side, I blew her a kiss. I missed my eight-year-old princess. Junior tried to put his hand against the glass, but he was too short. Mom lifted him and I put my hand on his, hoping he could feel my touch through the glass.

Tania held him on her hip. "What is gonna happen now? How long are you going to stay here?" Junior fidgeted, tapped on the window, and looked from me to her.

"I don't know, but the food is much better, and it's a good break from that Hell."

"Yes, I bet. I hope you get well soon. We'll come to see you next week, okay?" She smiled, but her eyes said something else.

I felt her heart sailing away.

I wish I'd died at the operation, I can't take this anymore. "Okay, I understand if you can't come...don't worry, I will be fine." We prayed, and they got ready to leave.

"Bye, love you." She told the kids to wave good bye. They all smiled and looked happy to get out of there.

I didn't blame them, I could tell they didn't want to come, and they were eager to leave. They didn't come back to the hospital.

After a few more weeks of observation, and the catheter still draining yellowish fluids, I was transferred back to jail.

Classification assigned me to a one-man cell area of the Main Orange County Jail. It was the housing area for the "high power" inmates -Red Banders, for the red ID wristband-troublemakers, known gang leaders, or psychos.

I looked at the Deputy in charge. "I need to go to Shelter Living, Sir."

"No. You have been classified to come here, and here is where you are going to stay." He stepped closer as I, and another four inmates lined the wall. "Why are you here? What did you do?" His voice rose and his nose a few inches from my face. Spit peppered me.

"I have been advised by my attorney not to discuss the nature of my case. It's all in your computer, Sir."

He moved to the next inmate and continued yelling, then, opened the door to the cellblock. He pointed at me. "Go to your cell. Tomorrow put in a medical slip to see the doctor."

I walked inside the cellblock. Other inmates cursed, whistled, and yelled obscenities. Thick tattooed arms grabbed the bars and bitter faces followed my every step. The tank had two tiers, and the inmates on the second floor motioned and signaled in the reflection of the catwalk's tinted windows. I walked into the one-man cell and the door, activated by the officer, slammed behind me.

I sat on the bed.

"Hey, you have to pay taxes to stay here." The voice came from the upper tier.

"Who do you run with?" Another, seeing in the glass wall's reflection.

"I am Colombian."

"Coca?" A third cut in.

"Si."

"Got connections?" The voice from the top tier took a different tone.

"Busted, too hot now." I spoke with a growl.

"How much they got you with?"

"Five hundred kilos."

"You're goooone, big dog."

"Thanks. Homey. They wanna give me fifty-four. I need to get back to medical. I just came from the hospital." I stood against the bars. "Can somebody call the deputy, I am bleeding."

"Deputy, deputy..." The voices carried down the tank. "Man down, man down..."

"What's going on?" The P.A. thundered.

"Man bleeding." Several guys shouted. Usually meant someone was dying on the floor.

"My surgery opened, and it's bleeding." I waved my arm through the bars.

"Okay. Roll it up." The door opened.

I took my bedroll and walked out. "See ya..."

"Keep in touch, Colombia." One waved. "I'll see you in court." My new connections yelled from behind me.

"Sure..." I walked out and breathed thinner air. Grin.

"What's wrong with you?" The deputy stepped out of his office and growled on my face.

"Bleeding. My surgery busted open and it's bleeding." I lifted my shirt and pointed to the soiled gauze.

Suspicious eyes glanced back, and then he spoke into the

mike pinned to his shirt. "Need escort to medical."

The medical area of the Main Jail looked normal, until I was taken to my room. "I waanna know what love is…I want you to show me…." Someone sang over and over. Howling and screams echoed through the otherwise empty corridors. Then, I was shown into my new accommodations. The room had three beds. One was occupied by an old white man, and the other by a young Mexican. I walked to my bed and sat. "Hola." I waved to the Mexican. We talked about the programming –schedules and rules- of this area of the jail while the white man slept. I spend most of the time reading my Bible as I recovered my strength.

After the catheter was taken out and the incision closed, I sent a request for transfer out of Shelter Living. It took another week to see the doctor and get cleared for general population. Finally, I got transferred to the I.R.C. –the Intake and Release Center area of the jail- again.

Being back in the two-man cell was a relief.

Months passed, all kinds of tests came, my faith continually attacked by sickness and loneliness.

I also suffered from gout -a painful inflammation of the lower joints, usually the big toe- and during the incarceration period I also got it in an ankle, knee, even an elbow. It was so painful, and usually it took two or three days to get medical attention, by then I felt like cutting my leg off. The symptoms were some discomfort of the joint, warmth, and stiffness, then by the next day, swelling and excruciating pain. The pain throbbed up the bone, and it pumped distress into my brain to an unbearable estate of mind.

One time, I had gout in my knee. Late that night, I called the officers through the intercom so many times they finally let me go out of my cell, and trade a jar of coffee for pain medication. An Asian guy, two cells down the row reluctantly pushed a purple capsule under the door. I limped back to my cell, took it, and woke up the next afternoon.

Gout. For some people it's a matter of diet, but for me it kept coming back when the stress level went up. The court appearances every two or three months, the Feds' interest in my case, the riots in the dorms, the transfers within the jail, and the family matters, especially the financial difficulties of my wife and children, catapulted the sickness. Calling home collect had become expensive and depressing. There was nothing I could do for them. Between jail issues, house issues, and gout issues my life became a constant prayer.

Pain brought a new vision, I couldn't even read or concentrate, but it gave me a clearer picture of what Hell could be.

Regardless, the legal process continued month after month, court dates postponed, new evidence and discovery analyzed. I pressed my attorney to find out how the Anaheim Police Department detectives had found me, to press for the detectives to come and testify, but no answer was given. Finally, the judge said that they were not the ones on trial, I was. The prospect of going to trial represented more attorney fees which compounded the financial pressures.

After burning through the savings and selling all that was not bolted down, my wife, who had no business experience, panicked about the future. I suggested selling the house and investing in a dance studio, since she was a professional ballerina. My financial projections showed that within two years the studio would provide enough to support the family, and later to buy another house.

She didn't follow that plan. After selling the house, she bought a condo in addition to opening the studio. Now she didn't have capital to support the studio until it produced the projected income. Then, she took out a loan on the condo, and after months of struggles, lost it all. The only avenue now was to trust God to get them through the hard times, and hard times came.

After nearly three years in jail, I had to face the Day of Truth. The prosecution offered 14 years for each of the three charges. My attorney brought the offer on paper but it said 22 years. He explained that it had to be drawn like that. It devastated me, but with no choice, I signed. At court, I pled guilty.

The sentencing date approached like a stormy cloud. Five weeks of faith versus fear. I prayed and prayed, but terror filled me. Finally, the day came and the judge sentenced me to forty-two years total, fourteen years for each charge, to run concurrent instead of consecutive. Praise the Lord! It meant that, minus four years credit for time served, I had only ten to go. Since this was my first felony conviction, I would serve half of that. I only had five more years of incarceration, out around 2004 instead of 2024. Hallelujah!

My wife wanted me to take the case to trial and I laughed at her ignorance. There was no chance of winning, I'd get the maximum sentence for each case and they'd run consecutive. Almost seventy years sentence, to serve thirty-five. However I did the calculation, it would be much more. Besides, Cruces testimony alone would convict me. What I didn't know was that he was already dead. The Feds had given him three years, let him out for good behavior, and deported him. Ha –what a burn. *I told ya...*

I had a good attorney but he wasn't God. He wasn't in the miracle business. God came through for me, and if I needed to do the time to change my ways, I was going to do it with Him by my side. Besides, like the saying goes, "If you can't do the time, don't do the crime." No bad deed goes unpunished. Some people are fee but they do their time in their minds –looking over their shoulder- which is the worst prison of all. Others are prisoners of their own scheme. To me, it couldn't get any better than that, only five more years to serve.

After sentencing, I waited to "catch the chain." I didn't know why they call it like that, but soon found out. I was used to being chained going to court. Shackled, handcuffed to a chain around my waist, and feet tied with a short chain, but this time I would be shackled to another inmate. Sometimes the wait for the chain could be months. For me, it took a couple of weeks.

I was in the dayroom reading when I heard the announcement. "Rausch, roll it up." I was going to prison. Everyone said that State prison was much better than county time. I couldn't understand it, and to me it was still horrible. I told my cellmate to call my wife collect and tell her about the transfer. I had no idea how long it was going to be until I could call her again.

19 THE FREEDOM

The trip up to the California Central Valley was my first taste of scenery. Some prisoners joked and made obscene gestures every time they saw a woman drive by. I looked out of the window, enjoyed the ride, and wondered what was coming next. At least I had a date to get out, and I hoped to stay alive until then.

Riding jail's buses brings an overload of information and feelings. People say and do the most stupid things –obscene gestures and things that made me sick. Sometimes, female prisoners would be on board and I'd reflect on the women in my life. During a trip to court, I remembered Tammy calling on god, and wondered what god she'd conjured. Gods I had, demons I fought. I'd been my own god and now, riding that bus to prison, I called on the true God to get me through what I deserved.

We finally arrived. Wasco State Prison, the reception center to the California Department of Corrections, CDC, had been in lockdown status for months due to riots. What would this be like? As we got off the bus and got in a holding cell, I eaves dropped. One talked about "The shoe." It would be great to learn to make shoes.

I piped up. "I want to go to the shoe."

They went quiet. I figured my interruption wasn't appreciated. Come to find out, it wasn't a shoe factory, but the SHU-Segregation Housing Unit-where all the troublemakers spent their time. Some inmates preferred that kind of housing.

It took the whole afternoon to clear Receiving, and then we were taken to the assigned buildings. The programming consisted of staying inside the building, and only getting out of the cell to the dayroom for a couple of hours to shower, phone, and TV.

The square building had the officer's tower at front, and two tiers of two men cells along the other three walls, with showers in the middle of each row of cells. In the center of the building there were several metal tables bolted to the floor with welded stools.

The most wonderful thing happened when the doors of the cell opened for dayroom the first time. I saw a group of inmates carrying their Bibles and setting up for study on the tables. I got mine and joined them. From far away the tattoos and demeanor blended, appeared the same as the rest, but when up close, these guys shared their faith and God's light shone in their eyes. It encouraged me. Some had strange theologies that gave me a taste of prison religion. Some believed that we didn't have to share our faith, God was going to save the elect no matter what. Others were dimming God's grace by adhering to rules and regulations, following the law, or trying to. The players, as I called other group, appeared to join to take advantage, exploiting, one minute speaking God's word, the next, cursing among the mockers. They asked for canteen and when I wouldn't share my limited supply - during transfers canteen access could take months- their common accusation was, "what kind of Christian are you?" getting my usual response, "A wise one." One even asked for my new MacArthur study Bible. Tania had purchased it and the Orange County jail chaplain had brought it in the day after my sentencing. When I wouldn't let the other brother take it to his cell, he got upset. Transfers could happen anytime and I could loose it. Besides, my belief was that sometimes God gave me a limited supply to administer properly (2 Cor.8:8-15), more so, in this case it was my sword, and only Satan wanted me without it. No, I am not saying that the individual was Satan, but if he had his own Bible, why would he pressure me to give him mine? Something made me suspicious. I enjoyed sharing my canteen, when I could, but what I cherished the most were those opportunities to share my faith, and that study Bible had come at the most opportune time (2 Cor.9:5-15; Act.3:6a). I had read a few versions of the bible in Spanish, and I wanted to read this New King James version cover to cover. It reinforced my faith and was the best way to spend my time.

After a couple of days, the reality of the prison term hit me. I complained to God feeling lonely and uncertain about the future. Then, my cellmate got transferred and I prayed for a tranquil one. He rolled in –literally- a few hours later. I felt sorry for myself no more.

He was about twenty-one years old and sentenced to life for a murder during a jewelry store robbery. He'd fled to another state and was arrested. During the extradition back to California, he'd attempted to escape and the police escort shot him through the chain link fence severing his spinal cord with the bullet.

I stopped whining and gave thanks to the Lord for my health, my short sentence, and my freedom. Feelings can change, and I praised God because my salvation was not based on my feelings, but on His love for me that didn't changed (Rev. 21:6-7; 1 John 1:5-9; 5:13). As I understood God's love, it moved me to analyze my bitterness and hatred against my father. Still, I couldn't reconcile or have peace. Just the thought of him made my blood boil. I was supposed to forgive but couldn't. I prayed and prayed for wisdom about it, about a revelation that helped me to overcome that rotting hatred.

Reading the Bible, praying, and exercising, along with the regular prison activities blended days into weeks.

After about a month, the lockdown ended and the prison returned to the regular program. I enjoyed the sunshine in the yard. Running on the track with a brother, we sang. "Nobody can trample with my mind because stays on Jesus."

I approached groups sitting on the grass, and asked if they wanted to pray. One individual mocked me. "Play? You wanna play?" They all laughed.

"No, pray, pray, you know..." I put my hands together feeling foolish.

"No, thanks." He waved me off.

Later that day, he knocked on my cell's door. "Hey, can you pray for my sister? She overdosed at a party last Friday. She is seventeen and...is in coma." He leaned his forehead against the door as tears rolled.

"Sure, let's pray."

Mockers need God the most.

Never saw him again. People got transferred all the time and when I felt the urge or call to approach someone, I did it. When I didn't, I regretted it, the next day they were gone.

I applied to be a *trustee,* so I could be out of the cell, get busy helping, cleaning and whatnot. The downside was that people asked me to take *kites* –notes-to their associates, and who knew what else was inside those folded little pieces of paper. My job lasted one day. I got transferred to Corcoran State Prison. On the bus trip to Corcoran I enjoyed watching the fields and the open spaces. I'd never looked at life that way before, enjoying every little thing.

It reminded me of a time my mom had come to visit from Colombia. As we drove, she commented on every little thing. "How pretty...oh, how beautiful...oh, look at that..." For her, everything was a joy then. That night, when we got home, alone in our room, my wife and I made fun of her. How sad. How cold a heart can get. I didn't appreciate anything then. Now, looking out of the prison bus' window, tears flowed. *Sorry Mom, for all I've made you suffer.*

At Corcoran, living with lifers was an impacting experience. Some of these men had been inside twenty, thirty years, and would never get out. It was too difficult for me to imagine, and though I had been close to receiving such a sentence, living there made me grateful and reinforced my trust in the Lord.

Respect was the number one rule, and when broken, someone bled. I met guys serving more that one life sentence and killing again didn't make any difference.

The shot-caller for the Colombians welcomed me, and asked me about my case. Usually if there were any doubts, the newcomer had to provide court records or any paperwork indicating their crime. In case of inmates in for rape, gang or mafia adjustments, the shot-caller would assign one of the lifers to cut the newcomer's throat. Some targets came to the yard with "green light" tagged to be killed. Information traveled fast in the prison system, in those cases, faster than their transfer.

The shot-caller explained the rules and politics of the system. Which showers to use -there were six, and their use was separated by race- even seating at the mess hall was enforced. This system was supposed to reduce problems and friction. Basically the main rules were to respect others and keep out of other people's business. If a problem arose with someone from another race, I was to go to him to negotiate an agreement. Failure to reach one usually ended in a riot.

Seeing so much hatred exposed mine. I prayed to understand and remove those rotting feelings against my dad to no avail. It tormented me, being a Christian, knowing about God's love for me, but not being able to heal that area of my life. So I kept praying about it, every time I thought about my father, I prayed that God helped me forgive him.

Seeing people living like animals in a cage, made me face my own prison. Hatred.

One day, a new inmate sat at the wrong table –a different race's- in the dining room. He was asked, probably not nicely, to get up and go to another table. He didn't. A fight broke out and later, when the yard opened, a riot between the two races erupted resulting in lockdown. Authorities investigated the source of the problem and transferred the persons in imminent danger. After a couple of weeks the races not involved went back to regular program–work, education programs, and yard. The races involved endured restricted program confined to their cells for nearly two months.

I continued my studies. After the Set Free Prison Ministries correspondence courses, I enrolled with Family Radio School of the Bible. This organization in Oakland, California, offered an Associate of Religious Education Degree. Studying the Bible kept me busy and out of trouble. I learned about God and my faith increased (Rom. 10:17).

Another Colombian introduced me to the Associate

Warden's clerk and he got me a job at the office. We were critical workers, and during lockdowns we still went to work. The AW and his secretary treated us like normal people. It was the best working environment in the whole prison. At the office, among people wearing nice civilian clothing, I felt free, almost living a normal life. Also, during the riot's lockdown, the shot-callers asked me to negotiate a release to regular program with the AW.

One morning, before my boss came to the office, I was using the copier, as a Sergeant came in. He approached behind me. I turned and he got close, too close, cornering me against a wall. "What did you hear in the yard about the riot? Are they going to go at it if we release them?" The big face was inches away.

"I don't know...they sure want to get back to regular program...you know..." I looked around and saw the Central Services Lieutenant glancing my way as she entered her office. *What is she going to think of this scene? Is she going to tell her clerks that I was giving information to the Sergeant?* One of her clerks was the yard's shot-caller for a major African-American prison gang.

"Are they going to go at it again?" The big Sergeant pressed.

"I know they want to get back to regular program, Sir, but, I don't get mixed in prison politics, that's not my thing." I tried not to blink.

He smiled. "Let me know if you hear anything." He walked out of the office.

I had to talk to the Lieutenant's clerks as soon as possible.

A month later, when the yard got back to the regular program, I was jogging around the track and saw the Lieutenant's clerks at their usual corner. Not missing a step, I trotted towards them. They were doing push-ups, training for war, and ready for anything. As I approached them, someone yelled behind me, and the shot-caller sprang to his feet.

I slowed to a halt. He recognized me and signaled someone behind me. I turned to see two young gangsters approaching rapidly. I faced the shot-caller. "Hey, whassup? You guys happy to be out?" I didn't want to look weak, so pretended not to notice my ill-timed approach, my breach of protocol.

"Hey, Colombia. Yeah, good to be out." He smiled as his huge paw engulfed mine and his glass eye looked sideways.

I turned to his friend, cell-mate and co-worker. "As-salamu alaykum." Peace be upon you -the Muslim greeting- shook his hand and bumped my right shoulder against his, as part of the salute.

"Wa 'alaykulum s-salam" Two rows of perfect teeth glistened.

The sidekick wasn't as big, but probably as dangerous. I feared the quiet ones the most. "Hey, the Central Services Sergeant was asking about you guys...what you wanted...I told him you all wanted back out." I looked into the shot-caller's good black eye.

"Yeah, I know. It's all good." Cold eyes, lots of teeth.

I never knew how to read these guys. Coming to kill me, they'd probably keep peeling their grill, all big smiles, as I bled to death on the floor. Nevertheless, the thing to do was to talk to him before he went to work the next day and spoke to the Lieutenant.

Life went on.

During my last year in Corcoran, on my birthday, I called

home. My wife told me she had moved in with another man, or he had moved in, the perspective didn't matter. Now I didn't have a family to look forward to anymore. The first months in prison, I'd readied myself for visit every Sunday. The PA announced, one after the other, "So and so, you've got a visit." Hours passed but there was no call for me. By now, I just hoped the new guy treated the kids well.

Around that time, my friend, the other clerk, transferred to CMC, California Men's Colony, an old military base and the country club of California prisons. He'd researched which prisons were the best.

My work position also helped me when it was time to transfer. After offering me to stay in the job there –which I politely declined- my boss asked me for two prisons where I wanted to transfer. At the year's classification review he put a word in for me and there I went also. Near beautiful San Luis Obispo, with coastal weather and dorm living, it made the rest of the sentence more pleasant, another blessing.

My sister came to visit once. She told me that Mom had lost weight and kept getting sick worrying about me. I had no solution to the family's issues, so I shared about God, and she accepted Jesus Christ as her Savior. How awesome that March 7th of 2000, she became my sister in Christ. I hoped mom also gave all her cares to God (1 Peter 5:7; Philippians 4:6-7). Poor Mom, all the misery in her life was my fault.

Remorse and guilt crept in, making me feel unworthy of the love of God. My feelings fluctuated, changed with moods, and were easily influenced. The Bible assured me that the facts which sealed my salvation didn't change because they were based on God, and He didn't change (Ephesians 2:8-9). My interpretation of scriptures became more accurate as I studied and listened to messages.

Not based on feelings but in facts, I continued sharing my faith with my family and anyone who wanted to hear about God. It frustrated me seeing Mom hardened to the message of salvation. Her traditions were based on rituals and images, not on a relationship with God. I didn't want her to die without understanding what Jesus had done for her.

"I ask and ask God to get you out of there, and He doesn't." She would say, over and over, during the weekly collect calls.

"Mom, God already helped me. Be thankful, and you'll see His blessings." I pleaded. "If you start your day giving thanks and recognizing what God has done for you, He will bless you more."

"No, God doesn't listen to me. How is the weather? Are you eating right?"

It hurt to hear her suffer. If she sought God, He could help her. I rested my head against the cold acrylic window of the phone booth.

The collect calls to Colombia were short and expensive.

At CMC, I worked at the Law Library where I learned to research case law and to type. After about a year I was re-assigned to a SAP, Substance Abuse Program, a pilot program mandatory to inmates with records of drug use. Even though I had stopped using since 1992, the initial interview for classification recorded that I qualified for the program.

Furious about the transfer, I spoke with my boss at the library, trying to override the transfer, but God had a plan. Time taught me that faith in God required understanding and acceptance that He was in control, and that He had the best in mind for me (Romans 8:28; Hebrews 11:1,6). Trusting in Him created a foundation for following His guidance (Proverbs 3:5-6). Knowing that God didn't change and reading about His love for me and all of His people, helped me to trust Him. He wouldn't betray me nor abuse me.

At church, we had a good fellowship in English and Spanish. I took music classes, joined the choir, and participated in plays. These fun activities broke the monotony and enlightened my walk with God (Hebrews 10:25).

I reluctantly left my comfort zone at the library to find that it was not a disaster. The transfer was a blessing in disguise and a ministry opportunity. About two hundred inmates participated in different recovery activities during the half-day assignment. The opening meeting had announcements and presentations. One was *The Theme.* I shared biblical principles without direct Scripture quotes, in order to comply with the rules. The story-telling at middle school and the stories I'd told day by day while living my criminal life, that gift now had a purpose. Looking at a bird fly over the prison yard became a *Keep It Real* theme, everything became a story. Scriptures in my overactive imagination created captivating and motivational themes.

That ministry was a beautiful experience, and gave me thick skin, exposing me to rejection like nothing before. *Keep It Real* was welcomed with "Oh, no, Jack again..." Moans and groans, but after a while, everyone joined me at the closing. "Let's Keep It Real."

The joy of writing presented me a perspective of God's plan that I had never considered before. While in Orange County Jail, I'd read over one hundred novels, took bible studies, and wrote numerous essays, creating a foundation for my new mission. Communicating God's works opened an awesome field without limits, and brought great rewards.

I accepted change as part the whole plan of God. What I often considered uncomfortable, even disastrous, like a job change, a business failure, or being in prison, turned out to be for the best, for His purpose. I learned the real meaning of Romans 8:28. "And we know,"-because I had experienced-"…that all things work together for good to them that love God, to them who are the called according to his purpose." Being called according to His purpose meant surrendering to His will and becoming His disciple, the true meaning of calling Him my Lord. I never imagined His plan would take me to the places and opportunities it had, or lead me to do the things I did. Ministry gave me a new life, a future and a hope, just as He had promised (Jeremiah 29:11-13).

When Jesus said to ask in His name and you shall receive, He was talking to His disciples, and this applied effectively when His purpose was in the disciple's mind. James 4:3 "You ask and do not receive, because you ask amiss, that you may spend it on your own pleasures."

The Bible became the center of my life. Learning, memorizing Scripture, or just reading it created a solid foundation for my faith. Practicing was the hard part, a daily battle. That struggle made me grateful to know I was forgiven and that by His mercy and grace He continued to forgive. His love motivated me to walk the talk, even though I often fell. I repented, got up, and continued following Him. I wanted to be the man of God He'd created me to be.

A counselor at the SAP program helped me face my past. It was important to overcome those experiences that still hurt, even though I didn't want to revisit those issues, or ever share them with a woman. Nevertheless, because of my issues, the Holy Spirit revealed to me all the damage and pain I had left in my wake. It was nearly unbearable to examine myself. It would have been easy to turn back then, but I realized it would be even more painful to continue in that old path with no future. The key was to allow the Holy Spirit transform me.

I faced those feelings the rape had embedded, and reconciled within myself my willing experiences. I tried to understand why my mind rejected what my body had felt. God had created me as part of a perfect plan. No matter what influences came into the equation, He could heal and restore my life completely.

I examined those areas of my heart, those feelings and emotions that I had never wanted to face before. Revisiting those hidden monsters, those moments of darkness, gave me the closure and helped me to recognize them as triggers for bad behavior. As I recognized and repented of my sin, I was able to detach the actions from the persons that hurt me and see the sin in their lives. How could I not forgive those that sinned against me if God had forgiven me? God forgave me because He loved me, understanding that love was the first step towards forgiving others. It was in my own best interest to forgive, though I would never forget. Forgiving healed me.

We are all sinners.

During this time, familiar and unfamiliar monsters waited for me along the way. Again my life unveiled those issues that, like the Trojan Horse soldiers, sprang out into my path. Still, as much as I tried and prayed about it, I couldn't forgive my father's abandonment and abuse. Hate didn't mix with God's love, as light and darkness, they can't coexist. I couldn't understand those feelings, but I kept seeking God for answers.

My criminal identity was gone. The Kamikaze, the Loco, the crazy Colombian was stripped of his mask. What were my choices now? I thought about becoming a veterinarian. Better to deal with animals than with people. I prayed about it and it didn't feel right. I remembered Jeremiah 29:11–God promised-"I will give you a future and a hope." I kept seeking (Matthew 7:7-8). *Keep It Real* helped me to set realistic goals vital for the future.

The Cross was the mark in my time line, a point of reference -my criminal past, my lack of purpose and direction now before my Savior- never to be forgotten. After The Cross, I could see a future in God.

Finally, after continual prayer, I understood my father's behavior. After nearly five years as a Christian, God revealed to me that my father had issues in his life he hadn't been able to cope with, turning him into a violent drunk. I'd lived the same path, and through prayer God revealed to me what it was. My father had bragged about parties and things he had done in his life, but I hadn't put it all together. What happened with my father came to a closure, now what was important was to heal and forgive so I wouldn't follow the same path. He had been a sinner just like me. I hated his sin and forgave the sinner. After all, hatred victimizes me first of all. Then, God showed me how He could use my past and pointed the way to a better future. Men shared with me about similar issues, and now I could help them seek God for healing also.

No child should suffer any kind of abuse, for it is a terrible thing that oppresses many women and men for life. Unless one allows God to intervene, there is no healing, and worse, the chain continues.

People came to me for advice and through the Bible we found answers. Prayer became a fabulous tool to help others draw near to God, and a vital communication with my Lord. I found the truth about Psalms that I had twisted for my own purposes. Like Psalm 18:19 "He -God- also brought me out into a broad place; He delivered me because He delighted in me." I interpreted it as if God was going to set me free because I had received Jesus as my Savior, and thereby I pleased Him. Instead, God had, in fact, delivered me from a life of sin through Jesus. That pleased Him and truly sat me free. I prayed about freedom and found out what real freedom was. Continuing in God's word, reading the bible, the only uncompromised truth, did set me free (John 8:31-32). My mind could be a faith crusher, but the Bible put it all in the right perspective. Rationalization had very little to do with faith. As a matter of fact miracles didn't make sense at all. I learned that God's ways were, much different than mine, and more fulfilling.

Victory over the enemy within became the main priority in my walk with God. I had become my worst enemy, and only through God's power could I experience that freedom and victory. It's not a matter of "I got it," it's a matter of living through it. It's not a matter of winning the battles, it's a matter of getting stronger through them. I could live for Him and be free of my own destructive behavior and desires, but I had to put, at least, the same effort into following Him that I had put into following my own desires. If I sought God as much as I had sought sex, I would become a spiritual giant. The problem was I still wanted sex. It occupied my mind constantly.

So I prayed.

I found scriptures about healing while the excruciating pain of gout throbbed in my toe or knee. Those scriptures and prayers worked sometimes to heal, other times they broke me and brought me to my knees, though not literately. There is no bending of a gout affected knee. Sometimes the only relief was to know that God had something better coming for me. The relief came from looking towards eternity with no pain, no tears, and no problems. I prayed scripture over my body and sought medical attention also. I knew God wanted submission of my body and I found scriptures related to that. I examined myself and asked for forgiveness in case the sickness was brought by sin and then prayed, "I am not worthy to receive You, but say a word and I shall be healed." Then, I read; John 1:14; Romans 12:1-2; John 15:16; Matthew 8:8b; Isaiah 53:4-5; Psalm 23 and 91, closing with Matthew 6:10. "Your will be done."

These were prayers and scriptures that helped me heal when my appendix burst at the Orange County Jail and when I went into respiratory arrest at CMC. When in the ambulance, the paramedic reading my vital signs, "So much over so much...you know what that means..." The other paramedic nodded. Yes, he didn't need to respond. I was peacefully dying. It was actually very comforting to know I was going to heaven. I prayed Psalm 23:4 "Yea, though I walk through the valley of the shadow of death, I will fear no evil, for You my Lord are with me. Your rod and your staff they comfort me." As I drifted into a peaceful state, joy surrounded me, I wanted to stop fighting it and just go to be with my Lord but, instead I asked Him to give me the opportunity to share about Him with my son.

20 THE ENEMY

Church fellowship filled the social void the mafia years had embedded in my soul. A social network I'd never had before, a congregation of like-minded people seeking God on their own terms. I tried not to judge anyone's relationship with God because mine was not perfect, instead I enjoyed finding new friends, common testimonies, miracles, and manifestations of the power of God which moved and encouraged me.

A brother that was serving a life sentence shared with me that one day he'd been called to go to court. "I don't have a court date, I am sentenced to life." He'd said to the officer. He went before the judge and his sentence was reversed. He had prayed, and God had set him free. Yes, it didn't happen to everyone, others committed suicide when things got tough. My friend told me, "Jack, I am going to live in a cabin in the mountains, where I'll never get in trouble again. God gave me a chance, and I'm not going to waste it."

"Yes brother, that is right, He gave you another chance…don't waste it."

Before the change of sentence, while at the maximum security area, he'd looked out of the window and saw a flower growing between the concrete cracks of the floor. He'd prayed, "Lord, I wish to be in a garden again…" After the reversal, he'd gotten transferred and assigned to take care of the garden surrounding the Sergeant's office. God had let him know, step by step, that He was listening and will be with him all the way (Jeremiah 29:13; Joshua 1:5-9). He did it for my friend, He did it for me, and He will do it for anyone because He promised to. My friend still had to serve a few months, but from life to a few months, was a miracle.

The best miracle of all was my salvation.

Miracles.

One Friday afternoon back at the court's building in Santa Ana I shared scriptures with a young man while waiting for my court appearance. He accepted Jesus as his Savior and after the prayer he joked, "I would love to have pizza tonight Lord."

I looked at him. *That'd be kind of hard since you aren't going anywhere soon.* He was in a lot of trouble. I was called to court as an officer came by the holding cell and asked for volunteers to help with the moving of some furniture. I had never seen that happen before. He volunteered, and as a reward he ate pizza. That was a pizza miracle. God had let the youngster know that He was listening.

When I felt abandoned and alone, God reached out to me in ways that brought me to my knees filled with gratitude. Those Christmases with cards from only my mom and sister, I got letters from churches letting me know that God was present outside, and working beyond what I could see or believe.

One of those letters was from Calvary Chapel. They participated in *The Angel Tree Program*, an organization that collected and delivered presents to children of prisoners. I filled the form with my children's information and they got presents "from me" many Christmases.

Once, I received a card asking me for updated information about my children. They had tried to contact them, but the address on the form was not good, they'd moved. I sent the new address, and later on got a card telling what my children had gotten that Christmas. That was awesome.

That was God's love in action. I found those gifts moving. Someone out there had done an act of kindness without expecting anything in return. Like Deputy Lyons sharing scriptures the day I was booked, these people with *Angel Tree* were continuing the message of love into my healing heart. Showing love, and pointing the way for me to follow.

I looked for opportunities to share my faith with my Colombian friends, knowing that some searched for the real thing, but that many would miss it, mock it, and rebel against it. The majority, sadly, planned to continue doing the same things that got them in trouble, but the few that listened will live in my heart forever.

After more than a year in the SAP program, I signed up for a residential drug treatment that provided a place for me to live until I got a job. Now I just had to wait for my date with freedom.

Three months before my release date, I was sitting in a group session at the program when the head counselor came. "Jack, you are needed in the director's office."

"What did you do now?" One man elbowed me.

"You are in so much troubleeeeee." Another joked.

I stood, reluctant. I had gotten in some trouble for sharing scripture before, but never had been called to the director's office.

I followed the counselor, and he opened the door for me.

"Hi, Jack. Sit down please." The director pointed a chair.

"Thanks. Good morning, Sir." I sat as instructed.

"Jack, we are considering a few participants to be released early into a State Recovery Program. Would you be interested?" He leaned forward.

"Am I interested in getting released early?" This was no place for humor, I knew that much. "Yes. Of course…When?" I leaned forward. I couldn't believe it, I was a troublemaker according to their rules, but here they were choosing me, the first one, of two hundred, to go out early and into the pilot program, "Where do I sign?"

A week later, I was transferred to the prison in Chino, and a few weeks after that, to the program in Anaheim. There were six participants living in the four bedroom house and some were on the way. The next day, I was summoned to see the in-house Parole Officer. What a surprise to find Tania, my wife, chatting with her in the office. After the greetings, she served me with the divorce papers. I'd intended to work on the marriage but now it was too late.

After completion of the program in Anaheim, my sister picked me up with her husband and took me to a hotel. That evening we went to a mall. The abundance of colors and people walking around, children yelling and running, so much activity around me, made me crave to return to the hotel. I spent the weekend with them and then they took me to the residential program I had chosen while at CMC. All paid by the California Department of Corrections, because of my participation on the SAP. As a condition of my parole I attended recovery groups and Alcoholics Anonymous meetings. The AA meetings got my attention because these people stuck together.

I visited local churches with the program's house manager, and then I found the Christmas card from the Angel Tree program from Calvary Chapel. I came a few Sundays and found a bunch of easy-going, Bible-believing people who treated me like one of their own. I felt at home.

The preaching fed me. God had a way of bringing growth and paving the path when I was willing to obey. It was not easy. As a matter of fact it was painful and when I ignored His guidance, I suffered. Doing what I knew didn't please the Lord made me feel disconnected from His protection and blessings, and also brought back the old cloud of doom. Nevertheless, the cycles of disobedience, chastisement, and returning to Him, produced strength, produced a strong desire to be in peace with God that was stronger than the desire to do whatever separated me from Him (Hebrews 12:11;1 Peter 5:10). The process was awesome, supernatural, powerful, and obviously, unknown to the ones who chose to continue in their own path. Life had a flavor that only spiritual food could bring.

It was the best thing that could have happened to me. Yes, I still desired sex, money and power, but at the end of the day, I recognized that those things never brought what God had brought into my life. I also knew God would provide for my needs in His time, because He had promised it in His word, and because He had done it already in so many ways, one of them, the residential program where I lived (Psalm 23:1).

Between church activities and the recovery program my transition to life as a free man was much easier. Through the AA meetings I found a job. That morning at the meeting, I had spilled my coffee and as I cleaned it up, one of the guys struck up a conversation with me. He owned a flooring company and was going to do some measurements for a project the next day. I offered to go with him. He liked my proactive approach and hired me. I delivered the huge rolls of carpet and crates of tile to job sites, and also helped with demolition and whatever needed. The job was brutal, and at the end of the day every part of my body hurt. Trying to keep up with the younger men of the crew made the job a seemingly impossible task, so I prayed constantly just to make it through the week. We worked nights and even Saturdays because it was when the buildings were empty for us to replace the carpeting. Sundays weren't long enough to rest.

In the meantime, with a grant from Federal Student Aid, I enrolled in online classes at Saddleback Community College towards a business degree, and bought a car. Motivated by the program counselors' example, I changed my major to Psychology.

At the end of the mandatory period in the residential recovery program, I moved out, and rented a room in Aliso Viejo, near where my son lived. Now, with a car, a job, and a place of my own, things shaped up. I used part of the grant to take the practical training towards a commercial driving license. Driving big trucks became one of my goals, as some participants of the SAP program –while in prison- had given the theory classes.

During the training, one of the instructors offered me a job bringing one thousand kilos of cocaine from Mexico for one hundred thousand dollars. It was tempting, but there was no money worth spending another day in jail. Not to mention that crossing state lines or the border, would be a Federal crime with a life sentence for that much product. He said he was going to do it. I tried to convince him not to, but after a couple of weeks I never saw him again.

I rather drive for life, than do life for driving loaded.

I loved those huge machines. For my first job, I drove "Bottom Dumpers" –the tractor pulls two trailers with a clam shell type dump gate in the belly of the trailers. I carried gravel for the street's base of new housing tracks. The job reminded me of my off-road driving days back in Colombia, but much better. Now I laid foundations.

Work stopped when the raining season came, so I took a job picking up food donations. Through that job, I made a connection to drive regional, all over California. I told my parole officer about the job –as required by the conditions of parole- and went on my first trip. On the next weekly report to my P.O., she went ballistic. I wasn't supposed to leave the fifty mile radius from my place of residence. I guessed she wasn't paying attention when I told her. After some begging, and based on my good behavior, she allowed me to continue, but I had to call her every time I went out of town and back. I reported, even at one or two in the morning. The next time I saw her, she told me not to call anymore. "You didn't have to call me at three in the morning." Her eyes held a spark of humor.

I continued my online classes, and things were going well, until I fell into one of the enemy's terrible traps.

One of the participants of the drug program showed me how to search for pornography on the internet, and now that I had my own place and a computer, I started visiting those sites filled with soul-rotting materials. The old habit returned with vengeance. The old video tapes had been replaced by on demand non-stop videos. I found myself compromising my beliefs and going down this path of filth and misery. Pornography robbed me of the joy of being free and put me back in my own dark place, a prison I carried with me.

The images in my head polluted my whole life. Sometimes

I felt as if women knew about all the garbage I had in my mind. There is a passage in the Bible about God showing a prophet the inside of a room which walls portrayed idols. It was the heart of His people filled with what they thought they could hide from God, what they did in the dark (Ezekiel 8:1-12). Those were my idols. My heart's walls were covered with images that gave me pleasure, but were horrible in the eyes of God. Those images grieved the Holy Spirit within me.

My spirit battled this bodily pleasure. A similar feeling had tormented me after the rape. A part of me wanted to accept what happened, but my mind, conscience and feelings rejected it. Now it affected my spiritual life, hindered my relationship with God, like a computer virus, spreading, multiplying, corrupting, carrying darkness into my soul, and the source appeared to have no limits. This rotten pleasure, if I could call it a pleasure, moved into my life and got settled. It took me for a wild ride. The Holy Spirit convicted me. These acts of rebelliousness, this sin, contrasted with the joy of being at peace with God and enjoying His presence. It depressed me to know that somehow this habit had become more important than the One who died for me and had blessed me in so many ways. He had set me free, and I had walked back into the worse prison of all, the one in my mind.

The struggle crippled many opportunities and hindered my effectiveness to minister to others. Still, God showed me that He wanted to use me, but I was limiting His light into my life by playing in the dark.

After being an usher, handing out bulletins and helping people find their seats, at Calvary Chapel for a few months, I continued looking for ministry opportunities. Believing that church involvement would force me into obedience, and having the experiences I did, I started *Freedom by the Truth*, a recovery program at the church. Some of the participants preferred the

Alcoholic Anonymous format, but I believed that God, my higher power, was the only One that could set us free, and that is what I preached, preached, and preached. I believed that AA worked, and admired their dedication. It all reinforced my call to preach His Word. God had given me abilities, spiritual gifts (1 Corinthians 12:1-31; 2 Peter 1:3-4), and even though my vision for ministry wasn't clear, I continued to pray for guidance. This also helped me realize that Psychology wasn't my call, at least not for now. I loved to preach. The program grew for a while but then it dwindled to two participants.

Pastor Chuck Smith taught, "If the ministry doesn't grow, let it die with dignity." Nevertheless, frustration grew. I wanted to keep pressing forward and not feel like a failure. It became about me and what I could do, not about God. The dilemma brought me to realize that my victory couldn't depend on what I did for Him – how many programs I participated in, or how involved I got in a ministry. Victory had to depend on His love for me. I needed a supernatural weapon against a supernatural enemy. Satan's tools couldn't be underestimated.

There are no failures in the Kingdom of God. He didn't make mistakes. I'd pushed to make it work. I'd pressed too far, and finally realized that God wasn't in that program with me. God guided me, but somewhere along the way I had taken a turn. Yes, I'd taken a step of faith, and through it God showed me that *I was usable,* and He also showed me my ulterior motives. I wanted to be an instant success, here *I AM.* God showed me that it was not about who I am, it was about who He is, and about being in fellowship with Him, in harmony with His will. He made things happen, He gave and He took away (Job 1:21).

After that ministry closed, at a men's dinner, I had *a revelation,* and after praying about it, presented my new idea to the pastor. On 7-7-2007 I suggested to the pastor a Hispanic Ministry.

He said. "Go for it." He was going on vacation, and told me that we would talk about it some more when he got back.

I confess, when I believed God was calling me to do something, I charged and left Him behind. After I prayed about it, and when I believed that a confirmation came –"Go for it."- I ran with the idea without continuing to trust and ask Him for guidance.

When the pastor came back from vacation, he and the church board suggested I enrolled in the School of Ministry, so grudgingly, I did. I had a four-year degree, seven years of study – my correspondence courses in prison- and experiences that I believed were enough training. Oh, how wrong I was.

La Escuela de Ministerio –the Spanish version of The Calvary Chapel School of Ministry turned out to be the best decision in my life after receiving Christ as my Savior. The courses prepared me in church administration, expository preaching, and most importantly, self-examination. The battle was so fierce, Satan's opposition so vivid, I knew this training had been ordained by God. Every step toward God counts. No matter how many times I fell, I continued to get up and hang on to my Savior.

By now, God had blessed me with my own truck. A coworker was going to sell his tractor and leave the company, so instead I offered my services as a driver because his truck was much better that the one I drove. He suggested giving me his tractor and pay it as I worked it. He gave me a $25,000 dollars truck, no down payment, nothing. Yes, God was in the miracle business. I had prayed many times to become an owner-operator. A week later we signed the papers.

This new enterprise drew me closer to my Provider as nothing before. I needed eight hundred dollars a week for diesel alone. My sister lent me for the first trip. I went to Sacramento, unloaded and picked up a load. Driving down, as I stopped at a rest area to sleep, I tossed and turned worrying about where the diesel money was going to come from for the next trip. I begged the dispatchers of the company to advance me *my money* so I could fuel. It enraged me when they gave me a hard time, but it brought me to my knees, crying to the Lord to give me understanding. *Thank You for the truck Lord, but would you provide for the fuel…and the tires…and…and…and…* How humbling.

As the Hispanic Ministry required more of my time and while going to the School of Ministry –SOM- I changed from regional driving to making local deliveries. The classes were three days a week, 6-10 pm. Some days I got out of class and had to be at work at three in the morning, work until five in the afternoon, and to class again. Truck breakdowns, problems at work, and family issues made me consider, more than once, quitting the training. By the end of 2008 the trucking industry suffered greatly due to the rise of diesel prices and decreased work. To start the New Year, I needed more than three thousand dollars for tires, licensing fees, and repairs, so I decided to sell the truck.

Praying about the future, God gave me the idea to start the jewelry business again. I had some tools Tania had saved from the jewelry studio. I spoke with Gerson, my friend and director of the SOM, about the project. "This makes no sense. With this economy, making jewelry doesn't sound like a good idea." I slumped on his office couch.

"Jack. Miracles don't make sense, just trust God," my professor assured.

We prayed about it. Gerson always gave me wise counsel. I'll never forget my instructors at the SOM. They were patient and gave their time and knowledge to make me a better person. Ministry or not, the SOM changed my life forever.

Trials came and went. I invested the money from the truck in tools, and organized a working area in the bathroom of the studio I had rented. Could jewelry support me through the last semester of the School of Ministry?

21 THE WALK

The pressure was almost beyond my limits. It was frustrating to rely on faith for my income, I never knew if I had enough to cover future expenses. I prayed constantly about this plan of God for my life. Besides, I felt like people around me, including some pastors and teachers were just waiting for me to fold, to go back to my old ways. In addition to the trials, and I didn't completely understand how, but I knew that Satan had ways to confuse me. Nevertheless, the doubts, financial hardships, and sicknesses, turned out to be all a great blessing. I learned to trust God. It's a supernatural process, reading the scriptures about a particular need gave me confidence about His provision. From each of those trials, came real-life examples to share in the ministry.

Preaching was a serious commitment to me. The dedication to the school correlated to my call. There were spiritual gifts, but there was also a process. Delivering a well-prepared message was a great responsibility.

Starting the ministry involved doing everything myself. The congregation of the Hispanic Ministry suggested what needed to be done, but nobody wanted to do it. Egos clashed and personalities were sometimes hard to deal with. I led that ministry for two years while going to the SOM. I did it all still struggling with pornography. Listening to the teachers talk about being a leader and living in the spirit, emphasizing living a pure life and setting an example, ripped my heart. The garbage filling my mind oppressed me. While in my heart I wanted to please God, I couldn't understand that duality within me. I loved God but did things that I knew didn't please Him. One Sunday, before the service, I sat in my car and cried. I had to preach, but didn't feel worthy of doing it. Feeling like a hypocrite, I delivered the message, knowing I was limiting my effectiveness by my addiction. God used me, but I was cheated out of my full measure of usefulness.

The SOM brought more spiritual battles and many tests. The conflict was almost palpable, the enemy's attacks unbearable, but it was also a strengthening experience. Only through the Lord's love, mercy and grace, did I pass through.

God also opened the door for another ministry. I had told Him I would go *anywhere* to preach and do ministry, *except* to jail. "I will not go into a jail willingly, Lord." But, there is no saying "no" to the LORD. He taught me that if He was my Lord, there is only, "Yes, Lord." His will would be done whether I liked it or not.

One night during class, a guest speaker gave a testimony about jail ministry, and I felt God's call.

"Send *him,* Lord. Clearly he's the best for it. I am not going to jail ever again."

God spoke to my heart. "Yes, you are going to share in jail what I have done for you, just as someone shared with you."

I squirmed.

A notice posted on the school's board asked for Jail Ministry volunteers, so at the break I called the number. Nobody answered so I left a message. "See Lord, I was obedient." The class continued and I felt relieved until my phone rang.

I went outside. It was the Chaplain from Calvary Chapel Costa Mesa in charge of the Santa Ana Detention Center's ministry. I explained what God had told me to do, and shared my background. He told me he'd try to get me approved, and then asked how I'd known about his ministry.

"There is a notice here at the School of Ministry asking for volunteers."

"I've never put a notice there." He gathered my information, and hung up.

A couple days later I interviewed with the Sergeant in charge of the religious programs of the jail and I was approved. Amazingly, I now looked forward to sharing with the prisoners. Obedience paid a big return. Many of them received Jesus as savior.

The guys were thrilled to hear someone who had gone through a similar experience. A few troublemakers tried to sabotage the service, but after telling them that we were serious about seeking God and appreciated their respect, their attitude changed.

Ministry gave me great joy, but the struggle with pornography and lust really affected me. Determination to have victory brought periods of obedience that showed me how great life could be. Then, rejection, frustration, or whatever, triggered a fall and brought me back to that dark place. I knew deep in my heart that God wasn't pleased even though I could see Him working through me. I was robbing God by not giving Him my total dedication.

It tore me inside to live this double life and I begged God for strength to overcome my bad habits. I couldn't understand why I knew in my heart what was right, and preached about it, but I couldn't practice it. I tried every tool presented in Scripture, read books, and sought counseling. It tormented my soul to do things that I *knew* didn't please the Lord. I found some comfort in reading chapter 7 of the book of Romans where Paul shares about his struggles. Then, Romans 8:1 "There is *now* no condemnation to those who are *in* Christ Jesus, who do not walk according to the flesh, but according to the Spirit," relieved me. The comfort quickly fading as the last part of the Scripture downed on me, I was walking in the flesh, and I needed to learn to walk in the Spirit.

22 THE RESTORATION

Continuing the ministry, I surrendered my struggles to God. Galatians 5:16 says, "I say then: walk in the Spirit, and you shall not fulfill the lust of the flesh." The apostle Paul talked about the struggle between the flesh and the spirit.

It convicted my heart, and I continued to seek God for answers, continued faithfully following my Savior, continued reading and sharing the Word of God, regardless of my shortcomings. If I wanted to be used by God in the way He had appointed me to, I had to be obedient. As my subconscious ordered one foot to step in front of the other to walk, I had to listen to Holy Spirit to walk in obedience. I had to be aware of God's presence at *all* times.

Paul gives the Corinthian church instructions about that in 1 Corinthians 10:13. "No temptation has overtaken you except such as is common to man, but God is faithful, who will not allow you to be tempted beyond what you are able, but with the temptation will also make the way of escape, that you may be able to bear it." Also in 2 Corinthians 10:4-5, Paul tells us: "For the weapons of our warfare *are* not carnal, but mighty in God for pulling down strongholds, casting down arguments and every high thing that exalts itself against the knowledge of God, bringing every thought into captivity to the obedience of Christ." I wanted to practice those scriptures. I memorized them, and used them to build the strength to fight temptation, and *before* the fall, make a change, take another avenue. Turn the computer off, go for a walk, call my accountability brother, or take a cold shower. I did whatever took me out of that temptation. I tried it all, I read every book I could get my hands on, but, still, after a few months, I would fall again. I felt miserable, almost as miserable as when I was a drug dealer, but with a twist. Before I was miserable without a vision of joy, now it was worse, because God had given me a vision of freedom.

Regardless, God was faithful. His word let me know He was by my side. The key was to let go and let Him work in my life. Not to obey in my own power, or for my own reasons, but to let God do His work.

I gave up. I surrendered.

I wanted that freedom with all my heart and for the old habits to go away. 2 Corinthians 5:17 says, "Therefore, if anyone is IN CHRIST, he is a new creation, old things have passed away, behold, all things have become new." I felt like a hypocrite, living a play, and my mask wouldn't come off at the end of the day. Regardless of my feelings, I knew God could see behind the mask and into my heart (Psalm 149; Hebrews 4:12).

I'd met a good woman at the church and I thought she was the answer to my prayers. She was very charming, her smile lit up my night and her walk…well…she glided through the aisles of the church. I confused her smiles with interest in me. It did cross my mind that she could be playing me. But would a Christian woman do that? Nooooo. So, I courted her the only way I knew how. The Latino way. I flirted and joined the ministry team where she served. I wrote her a card telling her how beautiful she was, how attractive I found her. Well, she ran to the pastor.

I got a phone call. "Jack, could you come to my office tomorrow at ten?"

Hummm. "Yes, Pastor I'll be there."

The next day, the pastor kindly spoke. "Jack, you are gonna scare her away." He also questioned my approach.

"Hey, I just told her how I felt. No harm done. I'll back out." I tried to read into the chastisement. Did I do wrong? Why was I summoned to the office? Or, was he preparing me for this special woman, coaching me to be the "man of God" she was looking for?

Oh boy.

And we prayed, again, for the right woman, and the right timing.

I felt like a teenager without a clue of how to approach women.

It was frustrating, wanting to be honest and not play games, "waiting on the Lord," to bring the right woman. It also opened the door for the enemy to plant doubt and confusion.

"Lord, if she is the *one*, move her to seat by my side at the service." I prayed for a sign and the empty seat by my side didn't stop my weekly plea. Until one Sunday, I was singing, praising the Lord, and felt a presence by my side. I opened my eyes and there she was, with a hundred-watt smile. I closed my eyes again and prayed to say the right things this time so she wouldn't run to the pastor again. Nothing.

Why she chose to sit there that day I have no idea, but I waited patiently, tried to say the right things, and all the while she smiled, flirted and played. After a few e-mails, her choice, - why e-mail if we lived ten minutes away? Whatever- she wrote that I shouldn't be so open about my feelings, that it wasn't the right time, and that I needed to get my life in order financially. I felt like she wanted the old Jack, a player with money to burn. That woman broke my baby Christian heart.

Oh well.

While this infatuation went on, I managed to stay clear from pornography. But the change couldn't be motivated by people either. God's power had to be the moving force. He provided the tools, but the tools on an empty field didn't build the house. I had to clear the field by repenting, call on the Holy Spirit to fill my heart, and use the tools to build a solid foundation in Christ. I re-dedicated my life to the Lord often.

And, yes, many times I felt like giving up. When my criminal record prevented me from getting a job, when a relationship didn't work, when finances or health took a turn, I relapsed. I felt like there was no point in trying to keep doing the right thing, but the same criminal record, the memories of my past, all had created a point of reference. Remembering all the good things that God *had already* done for me renewed the desire to press forward pleasing Him.

I hated myself every time I fell, but if I could isolate the sin from myself, then I could bring the sin to the cross and offer my body as a living sacrifice (Romans 12:1-2). After all, I had to keep living for the call, the mission God had given me. When I focused on God, my problems slowly diminished.

In chapters 14 through 16 of the Gospel of John, Jesus

promised the Holy Spirit as my Helper. The book of John was specifically written to help people believe, and to believe is the work of the Holy Spirit in our hearts (John 20:31; 16:7-15). Jesus' letter to me assured His presence in my life, all I had to do was to read it and believe it. I had to confess that it was easy for me to believe in Him when He promised to save me (II Corinthians 5:17). Jesus gave His life for me and wanted the best for me and for every one who seeks Him by faith. (Hebrews 11:6) "But without faith it is impossible to please Him, for he who comes to God must believe that He is and that He is a rewarder of those who diligently seek Him."

I believed and prayed to Him for everything, big and small.

Finally, after struggling with the ministry and my flesh for two years, God closed the ministry. Jewelry supported me during the SOM courses and the Hispanic Ministry, but right after I graduated the jewelry contract was taken away and I started to look for a truck driving job.

No jewels, no tractor, no ministry, I hit a dry place.

Even though I had finished my parole, disclosing about my criminal record on job applications still prevented me from getting hired.

Finally, I got a job driving to Texas weekly. Announcing to the congregation that the ministry was closing broke my heart, but also relieved me. I needed to get well with the Lord. It was devastating to step down from the pulpit but I knew the reason. There was no discussion with God about it. I knew it was my compromising and disobedience. I knew there was no place for continual sin in the pulpit.

I drove through the desert every week for two years and prayed for an opportunity to get out of that job, to be able to attend church regularly, and hopefully get back in ministry.

In the midst of these battles, meeting other women helped me realize that my emotional connections were damaged by my inability to trust. My heart lacked the emotional connector. It made me vulnerable. The enemy is not fair, and does not follow the rules of engagement. Satan hit at my weakest points. My heart was broken again, and through it, I learned to wait on the Lord and to listen to that inner voice. I learned to override those urges and desires that caused me so much pain. I learned to choose the things that drew me close to God over the things that separated me from Him.

I learned to live for Him. He is all I need.

My joy and peace come from my relationship with Jesus.

I had victory. I love my Lord, for He has given me a new life. To continue in victory I must continue standing in His Word and enjoying His presence. Addiction changes faces but my Lord know them all. I surrender all to Him and in victory I'll walk.

God has given me a new family, His.

Only God knows the future, but one thing I'm sure of is that He is faithful. God is faithful and I will continue to seek Him and serve Him with all my heart for the rest of my life.

God has restored my life and given me new dreams to live for, He has given me a purpose and a hope, just as He promised.

Instead of chasing tomorrow's victories, I'll enjoy today's.

Rom 5:8 But God demonstrates His own love toward us, in that while we were still sinners, Christ died for us.

I have given my life; I have surrendered all to God.

If I am going to be controlled by anything or anyone, I rather be controlled by God, which is why I called Him Lord. He rules over me. I am not a slave of drugs, alcohol, or my fleshly desires; I am a servant and a soldier of God. I surrender to Him because I know He loves me and has the best in mind for me.

Would you do the same?

Would you seek God right now?

Would you let Him restore your dreams?

Would you let Him heal all your pain and relationships?

Would you let Him show you what true Love is all about?

Let all the praise and glory be to our Lord Jesus Christ.

THE END

Made in the USA
San Bernardino, CA
20 January 2014